A VENTURE IN IMMORTALITY

A
VENTURE
IN
IMMORTALITY

David Kennedy

COLIN SMYTHE
GERRARDS CROSS 1987

Copyright © 1973 by Colin Smythe Ltd.

First published in 1973 by Colin Smythe Limited
Gerrards Cross, Buckinghamshire
First paperback edition published in 1987

British Library Cataloguing in Publication Data

Kennedy, David, *1918–*
    A venture in immortality
    1. Spiritualism
    I. Title
    133.9′092′4   BF1277

    ISBN 0–86140–284–7

Produced in Great Britain
Printed and bound by the Guernsey Press Co. Ltd.
Vale, Guernsey, C.I.

Saraband for Ann
—for whom the dance is only beginning

There be many shapes of mystery
And many things God makes to be
Past Hope or Fear
And the end men looked for cometh not
And a path is there where no man thought
So it hath fallen here.

Last chorus of Euripides' *The Bacchae*

translated by Gilbert Murray

Contents

Preface

In writing this book I am aware that it combines a number of methods of approach to the problem of survival. The first two chapters are autobiographical and intended to be so. Their purpose is to sketch a relationship between two people, albeit briefly. The bulk of what follows is evidence concentrated into six to seven months following the death of Ann, my wife. These incidents are in my opinion neither trivial nor magnified in their importance. After twenty-five years in which I have made myself familiar with most of the serious literature on the subject of E.S.P. and the attendant question of survival of human personality, I at least claim that nothing is presented here which is vague or undetailed.

To the person reading this account who is not familiar with the methods of assessing detailed evidence in psychical research I would provide this guide. When you encounter specific detailed items of evidence—many of which items were outside my conscious knowledge, do not dismiss them as simply odd. Particularly in the many items where the information had to be checked by me later and verified. Recognise degrees of probability and after excluding any other factors as sources of information such as telepathy, deception, etc., look for first class probabilities.

If read and considered seriously, the serious reader will find himself faced with, I hope, another brick in the edifice which is slowly being built. This is the inherent probability that we survive the change called bodily death, in some form.

As a clergyman I am concerned to reflect on how all this experience relates to the position of orthodox religion today. Again I speak from first-hand experience of moving among bereaved church members and being aware of the poverty of any real belief in survival.

A quick note about mediums' fees: those that I have given

are the actual prices I was charged at the time. They may be slightly higher now, but of course they do not reflect present London rates.

Finally, I have attempted to introduce the reader to aspects of science and philosophy which have helped me, including surprisingly, some of the modern philosophers who would not have confessed to an interest in psychical research, such as Martin Heidegger and Ludwig Wittgenstein. Yet they have helped to clarify my thinking on the subject. Like every attempt to convey hope and belief at the same time, this book is tendentious. I have good precedents of Plato and St. Peter for this, both are concerned to plead a cause—to state with enthusiasm a belief and in the end to confess to 'a great hope' in the case of Plato (ἡ ἐλπίς μεγάλη) and in the case of the New Testament, 'a lively hope'. Yet both hopes are not divorced from reason. I trust mine is also attended by enough reason to persuade others to follow my lead and investigate the subject for themselves.

1

Once and once only in this life, I have had the experience of pouring out my heart to someone—before I thought to ask her name. This happened to me twenty-eight years and three months and seven days ago, when I met Ann for the first time. I was stone cold sober and she was equally so. It happened in wartime, in 1942, when the bombing raids literally moved Soho to Glasgow for a short spell. In a club called "the Centre" in Scott Street, in Glasgow—long since vanished. It was an art club—a ballet club—a poetry club and all the other combinations which made up the transient Bohemians' atmosphere of wartime Glasgow. At that time Glasgow had its refugees from Chelsea and Soho, its German and Austrian Jewish refugees and its cosmopolitan services population.

Here we met—Ann and I. I was twenty-six—she was twenty-eight. We literally recognised each other, although we were strangers. A lover is a transient thing, but the person you are destined to meet—is that person with whom in all the world you feel safe. There is a haunting passage of Scripture in Genesis in which Joseph in prison hears of the disturbing dreams of his fellow prisoners. "We have dreamed a dream, and there is none that can interpret it." And Joseph's urgent whispered reply—"Tell it me, I pray thee."

This is the secret of each isolated personality. We dream our dreams and look for that someone who will respond with the "Tell it me, I pray thee". Anyway, that is what Ann found in me and I found in her. We never spoke of marriage, or being engaged, or the formalities of courtship. I never proposed and she never accepted. We both knew that it would be strange not to live the rest of our lives together.

We were married on the 19th of September 1944. She suffered from fairly advanced heart disease—mitral and

11

aortic stenosis. She insisted on having a specialist's report before we married and the straightforward advice of the specialist was—no family. Even at that, the outlook was gloomy as far as a lengthy survival for Ann was concerned. A year after our marriage she began a succession of minor bouts of heart failure culminating in an alarming collapse and considerable degree of failure. At that time she had to be propped up on pillows at night and struggled for hours each night in the painful business of cardiac asthma. Finally the heart specialist whom we brought in ordered six months complete rest in bed and after that a regime of very limited activity. Pressed to make a prognosis to me privately, he said, "A year, maybe eighteen months". It seemed that our marriage was going to be shortlived!

At this time I was a consulting engineer—with no thought of ever entering the church as a minister. Indeed with no thought of entering a church *per se*. About this time I remember awakening one night with the clear sensation that I had heard a voice saying—"Ann will recover". It was 4 a.m. on a February morning. I felt as though a load had been lifted from my shoulders. In the morning the gloomy prognosis of a year to eighteen months of the heart specialist seemed as irrelevant and distant as a fairy tale. I knew she would recover and she did.

Ann grew in strength. We did things together which we never dreamed would be possible. Certainly she could never walk very far without breathlessness. But within these limits our life was exciting, thrilling. I think the greatest love of our lives was poetry. We seldom differed in our choice. The pleasure of theatre-going and films was intensified by the hours of analysis and arguing together. Together we discovered the majesty and the unutterable beauty of Socrates in the Symposium and the Phaedo. We read the tragedies of Aeschylus aloud to each other. We marvelled at the civilised wit of Aristophanes. But above all it was sharing—sharing—sharing. In art, in music, in drama, in literature, to see another person recognise a nuance and confirm an imagined effect—this is the greatest joy I have discovered in living, for it makes actual what is tentative. We had seven years of sheer bliss before the clouds were to gather again.

During all this time we shared an interest in psychical research. I believe the first step was taken by me. Shortly before we were married in 1944 Ann's younger brother Bill was killed during a raid over Germany. He was a rear-gunner and the plane with the whole crew was shot down over Belgium. There were no survivors. We spoke then about the possibility of survival. At that time Ann would have described herself as an atheist and she was also an ardent Communist. Looking back on it all now, I believe that period must have been a greater strain on Ann than I was aware of. Her parents knew that I was a conscientious objector and now her brother had been killed in a position of self-chosen danger, rear-gunner. Ann honestly felt that I was wrong in my attitude to the war but she saw that I was at least sincere and she never wavered in supporting my right to be a pacifist, even when she disagreed.

About that period I decided to have a private sitting with a medium, Mrs. Buchanan, long since dead. I said nothing to Ann of my intentions. How clearly I remember that sitting, more than twenty-five years ago. First of all this medium in light trance described the sound of being in a plane—firing—about to crash. "There is someone here, Bill. He is excited and he wants to get in touch with his sister. He says that before the plane crashed he and the others in the plane threw their wallets out of the plane." Presumably this must have been done so that if the coming crash resulted in everything being burned out at least their wallets with identification and more important any last letters or photographs they carried would be found.

Next, this communicator Bill said that he sent his love to *Giss*. This is most important because I had never heard of such a name before and I knew of no-one in Ann's family with such a name. There it was, and I wrote it down *Giss*. When I told Ann that I had been to a private sitting with a medium and that Bill had come through, she was naturally interested but the utter amazement was to come when I asked her if the name, *Giss*, meant anything. It turned out that *Giss* was the private nickname which Bill had at one time used for his younger sister, Mary. It arose out of some joke but as things do, it stuck. He always called her *Giss* and this was something I certainly did not know.

The other matter of the wallet was also confirmed, for it arrived at the family home many months later after the end of the European War. It had apparently been picked up by a farmer, some miles from where the plane crashed and kept hidden during the German occupation and later handed to the British authorities. The two items in the above sitting were enough to set in motion a keen desire on both Ann's part and mine, to find out more and more about this question of survival.

During the years which followed from 1946 onwards Ann and I had a considerable number of sittings with various mediums and the evidence pointing towards supernormal phenomena of some kind began to pile up. One may begin such an investigation with the presupposition that all mediums are either fraudulent, consciously or unconsciously and that there is a mixture of both. From this it may follow that acuity of observation and reasonable deduction could account for a great deal of what passes for mediumship. For instance, here is an imaginary sitting which could take place and which might give all the appearance to a credulous bereaved person, of genuine communication. First of all a booking is made in advance, with a medium. In most cases the genuine bereaved person is not concerned to hide his or her true identity. The booking is made in the genuine name of the enquirer. It may be that the booking is for a joint sitting for a couple. They arrive in their car at the appointed time. Let us assume a medium who is fraudulent in every sense. She is sitting at the window and makes a note of the car number, possibly with a Biro on her finger-nails. A couple who arrive together, man and woman, are usually husband and wife. She looks for the wedding ring. When a husband and wife come together for a sitting they have usually had a bereavement of some kind recently.

The medium may say, "I get a parent—someone's father. I get the name, William, there is also John and Mary and Margaret. You have had a setback recently. I see a break of some kind. I see a change in conditions. You have been worried about something recently. One of your parents is here—he talks about a car you have—the number is D.56-043. The clouds which have recently gathered over you will break. An aunt of the lady's with white hair sends her love."

This is an example of what any fraudulent medium could easily produce. There are a number of other variants. Something may be wrong with a clock at home. (What home doesn't have a clock which is keeping faulty time?) The important thing is to realise that this kind of mediumship is really rubbish as evidence. Yet it is quite possible for a person to come away from a sitting feeling that he has been given items of evidence when he has actually been given items of information which could fit a considerable number of cases. The important thing is to be very, very critical of all evidence. Deceptions may be conscious or unconscious but the genuine investigator into the question of survival does no service by being credulous.

The guiding principle is—look for specific, detailed facts and then submit them to the scrutiny of probability. What for instance is the probability of anyone else having a relative specifically named, who left behind a lucky penny in a purse unknown to you? Who had a blue box of talcum powder in her toilet bag at the time of her death? Who had four sets of dentures in the same toilet bag and a triangular bottle of toilet water and a blue slipper missing from her effects? These are specific items and the chances of them all fitting the same person are astronomical. If unusual names of relatives, like Teresa, or nicknames like Giss are also supplied then the possibility of fraud becomes so remote as to be non-existent. This kind of evidence can build up if an investigator is critical, serious and persistent enough. The question then becomes one of telepathy. Is it possible that unknown to the investigator, a great reserve of information acquired at some time is being tapped by the medium? The answer must be, it is possible! It has never been demonstrated that telepathy functions in such a detailed manner, but it is possible.

The next question is: What if information is given you purporting to come from a relative or loved one on the other side which is unknown to the investigator? This happens again and again in this narrative. The information then has to be checked from another source. If it is found to be correct again and again, this is very impressive evidence of an intelligence outside of normal bodily conditions, attempting to establish his or her identity. Finally, what if the information given is precognitive? What if the information can be demonstrated to be totally unknown to any human agency? In such cases the presumption of survival becomes very strong.

It was partly on the basis of such evidence that Ann and I reached the conclusion after fifteen years of intermittent investigation that we survive bodily death.

It would be tedious to detail the evidence of these fifteen years in this book. It is my intention to detail the evidence of six to eight months following the death of one of the partners both of whom believed in survival. How much solid, impressive evidence of survival can be arrayed in this short period, not in a life-time?

During this time I was an engineer concerned largely with electronics and my scientific training was in itself a useful preparation for the method of investigation which my wife and I shared. Firstly, one's own experience is important because it conveys an intensity and dramatic quality, one might say an existential quality to the problem. The "mineness" or, as the Germans put it, "Jemeinigkeit" of any position relating to our significance in the universe is important. Equally important is the reading of the best of the scientific evidence available. It is trivial to claim to have reached a conclusion on the question of survival without a detailed study of the best of the evidence pointing towards survival and also the best of the evidence pointing towards a possible alternative explanation.

Ann and I set out to do this over a period of years. Patiently we studied the volumes of the Society for Psychical Research Proceedings from 1906 onwards. Writing today as a minister of religion with considerable familiarity with most of what has been written from the theological and church centred viewpoint on this question, some things still surprise me. I know of no book by any orthodox theologian which examines in any detail the considerable body of evidence of cross-correspondences beginning in the Society for Psychical Research Proceedings from 1906 onwards.

The literary jigsaw puzzles claimed to originate from the minds of discarnate personalities, such as the Ear of Dionysius, which is perhaps the best known (see S.P.R. Proceedings, Vol. 29, 1918) are equally ignored by theologians. Also one might include the remarkable book-tests reported in the S.P.R. Proceedings, Vols. 32 and 33, 1911 and 1923. In these book tests the sitter is told of a particular part of a specific page of a book which is usually identified in its position in a book case in a certain room in a house where the medium has not been at any time. The message is usually claimed to come from a discarnate personality related to the sitter. This method is chosen from the other side as a means of producing evidence which excludes the possibility of telepathy. Usually the message contains words consistent with what the personality claiming to communicate would say to a loved one here.

These cross-correspondences, literary jigsaw puzzles, and book tests are slow and plodding material for anyone. Particularly this is so for the student who has to read the material in the Reading Room of a library which retains such material, in a large city or a University Reading Room. Nevertheless, Ann and I ploughed our way through everything of this nature and we discussed and argued the pro's and cons together over a number of years. In the end the personal, emotional and existential factors of our own experience with mediums plus the intellectual and analytical factors contained in the S.P.R. Proceedings, and the best of the other literature available brought us to the point of decision. We said, Yes! We believed in survival of human personality beyond bodily death.

It is significant to find Sir Alister Hardy in *The Divine Flame* part of the 1964-65 Gifford Lectures (Collins, 1966) make this statement: "Few dare to mention it for fear of being branded spiritualists, but there is in the publications and files of the Society for Psychical Research some very remarkable evidence (I am referring to the best of the cross-correspondences) which, I believe, if examined in a court of law, would be held to demonstrate one or other of two things: either the survival of some part of a personality, or a degree of telepathy with living agents, which is quite beyond anything yet demonstrated by the experimental method and, indeed, of quite a different kind. Such a finding by a court would not, of course, be proof acceptable by science to the reality of either, but it would point to something worthy of further research. Natural theologians must have the courage of those philosophers and scientists who, ignoring the possible ridicule and contempt of their colleagues, have risked their reputations to look at these phenomena."

We found that our friends who considered us soft in the

head or uncritical had never opened a volume of the S.P.R. Proceedings or read a line of Prof. C. D. Broad's works. Today, as a minister of religion, I find it strange that the best of the theological minds in orthodox churches appear to be in the same category. Prof. John Bailie's great and scholarly work *And the Life Everlasting* (O.U.P., 1934) is perhaps the finest study of what the title implies ever to appear in modern times (1935). No praise is too high for this work and I have read and re-read every page many times. Yet it is with a sense of sadness that I find even he dismisses all the evidence of survival which I have referred to in the S.P.R. *Proceedings* in these words, "An enormous mass of evidence has been collected in the Proceedings of the Society for Psychical Research and elsewhere, but it is enormously difficult to evaluate and interpret. The extent of the fraud that has been practised in this field is admittedly very great, so that there are many who doubt whether any authentic phenomena at all have been brought to light, while even those who admit the existence of the phenomena often think themselves able to suggest a simpler explanation of them than that of supposing them to be communications from the realm of the dead." At the time of writing these words all the evidence of cross-correspondences, literary jigsaws and book tests which claimed to originate from the other side was clearly published and available for study in the S.P.R. Proceedings. Whatever one may say of alternative explanations to survival suggested, and there are and were alternative explanations; no one could describe them as *"simpler explanations"*. They were explanations which postulated a hypothetical complexity and strangeness both in the human psyche and in the universe. On the principle of Occam's Razor that "entities are not to be multiplied without necessity" the survival explaantion was certainly the simpler one.

Yet to be fair to John Baillie he felt that "even if the spiritualists should turn out to be right, the result would have little bearing on the standing of our Christian hope." He may be right. But speaking as a minister who moves among people who are bereaved, each day, I am concerned that an awful lot of people lose their faith, break up and drift into pessimism and hopelessness at this point. To me this seems to have a bearing on Christian hope.

So Ann and I became convinced of the probability of survival. First from personal investigation, secondly from the best of the documented evidence. Thirdly from another source which is more difficult to define. At different times in our lives we were both aware of the exultation of certainty which comes as a deeply personal experience. For me the most vivid memory of my life is not an event in the workaday world but a fragment of a dream. This dream took place 22 years ago. In it I stood in the midst of a landscape in a morning mist, such as Turner might have painted. Only the colour was living and vibrating. My mother stood beside me and pointed out the beauty before me. I was filled with an incredible joy (my mother had been dead long previously). Strangely enough some art forms bring back a vivid recollection of this dream. When I listen to the last piano sonatas of Beethoven, particularly when I hear the high B of Op. 109 and the far away sound of something breaking through I get this certainty of joy and vibrating colour and the succeeding tranquility that all is well. There are glimpses of the same feeling of certainty and joy behind all appearances in Chekhov's *The Cherry Orchard*. Another time dimension seems to intrude and overshadow and again comes the golden landscape and the vibrating colour.

Ann was the only other person I have met who knew what I was talking about when I described this. Her certainty and sense of this other dimension of reality came mostly in art, particularly Vermeer of Delft. She could gaze on the "View of Delft" for hours and on a print of Monet's "Les Coquelicots" which gave her the same joy. I am particularly impressed by an observation of J. B. Priestley in his recent book *Man and Time* (Aldus Books, 1964) "I maintain that we are always taking what is in effect a four dimensional view of the persons nearest and dearest to us. It is in fact impossible to avoid taking this view in a close, deep and lasting relationship. We do not see these loved persons entirely in passing time, as three dimensional cross-sections of their real selves. We habitually see them, somewhat out of focus in passing time, in a curious blur that releases tenderness, not only as they are but also as they might be and as they were, reaching back, if we are parents, to their earliest childhood. The eagerness of lovers, and this is especially true of most women, usually more aware of this four dimensional effect than most men, to know, to see, what the other was like before they met, seems part of an instinctive desire to enjoy this deeper impression as soon as possible."

It is this four dimensional effect in life, this overtone to great art and music and literature, and above all to life itself as an art form expressed in profound tenderness and loyalty that so moved Ann and me to the awareness of a dimension of reality over, above and interpenetrating this life. The nature of the experience held its own validity and permanence, assuring us that nothing in three dimensional space, or in the uni-directional time series in which we live our day to day lives, could take it away. This of course, as I am well aware, is simply fantasy to the critic. But if the whole world were to stand against me and tell me that these experiences were really schizophrenic or pathological states I would still believe that the world was pathological and Ann and I were sane. In other words, I bet my life on the validity of these moments.

These three reasons confirmed in both Ann and in myself the belief in survival, and in what appeared to us by reason of our reading and experience of mediumship, the corollary of communication.

2

In 1951 the shadows gathered again over Ann's health. Her mitral stenosis, a degenerative process in some patients, reached a point again of breakdown in health and collapse and failure. Once more she was confined to bed, unable to breathe without difficulty and it seemed that our relationship at least in earthly terms was coming to its close. However, this was the period of the growth of heart surgery. Today mitral valvotomies are routine procedures in every large teaching hospital with a cardiac unit. Twenty years ago the operation was risky and involved, at least in Ann's case, three months or more in hospital.

After selection for this operation and tests, Ann had her mitral valvotomy and for a week or so looked like doing well. Then followed a pulmonary embolism, always a possible complication when a clot is dislodged from the heart following such an operation at that time. After another week or ten days of hanging between life and death Ann began to recover and grow in strength.

On an early spring afternoon in March 1952 I drove up to the hospital to take Ann home. She was so much improved in every way. At that time it was a miracle and she was radiant. It was certainly one of the happiest days in both of our lives as we stopped to admire the crocuses and sit in the spring sunshine. We even concluded our celebration by going to a cinema together. I felt that God had been good to me—beyond anything I deserved. It was that night, as in the middle of the night, listening to the relaxed, even breathing of Ann for the first time in years, that I made a decision. It was as though something snapped in my mind and a door opened. I would give up my lucrative and to me interesting work in engineering and go back to University for another five years and become a minister of the Church of Scotland. I felt that there must be some way in which God could use me, perhaps to bring joy, perhaps to share in the sorrow of other people's lives. Anyway it seemed clear that whatever the financial sacrifice, when so much is given back in a marriage, and for me Ann was given back, so much is expected and has a right to be expected from us.

I have never regretted that decision, nor did Ann. Once again we shared the excitement of studying theology and philosophy together. It was during this period that I had the second experience of the intrusion of another dimension of reality. One morning I awoke early, about 5 a.m., in mid-summer. Ann was still asleep. Suddenly, click! And I was seeing the bedroom and the world outside in a new dimension. I had risen and dressed before it happened. It was no dream. I was standing in the bedroom and everything was bathed in the same golden light of my previous dream. This time I looked down at Ann and around her head was a shimmering halo of the same intensified golden light. At the same time I felt an infinite, indescribable tenderness. A degree of tenderness which I had never known in my life before. An enhancement of all that tenderness had previously meant, towards Ann, and in a strange way, towards every living creature. Ann awoke, "I had such a strange, wonderful dream of being with you in a golden light," she said.

After five years at university, at the age of forty, I was duly licensed as a minister of The Church of Scotland, that was eleven years ago. A few months later I was called to be Minister of the High Kirk of Rothesay and parish minister of the Royal Burgh of Rothesay—normally a charge offered to a senior minister of considerable experience. We both felt apprehensive and yet excited as we started a new life on the lovely island of Bute, home of the ancient Scottish kings. The church of which I became minister had, in the late 17th century, been the ancient cathedral of the Isles and its history reached back to the 12th century.

For two years Ann was able to join with me in a limited way in the excitement and tensions of being a minister's wife. The whole reason and essence for the ministry today has always been for me the challenge of conveying in some way the Grace of God to people in need. This means all kinds of need. It also means getting close to people so that they can pour out their hearts to you and you can listen to them with the same concern that you would listen to someone you love. We fall short of this capacity to listen and capacity for warmth in many ways, but to try to convey God's concern to folks who have come to believe that nobody is concerned is the most worthwhile job I could ever desire to do.

After two years at Rothesay, Ann's heart showed signs of failure again and she went back to hospital in Glasgow for another operation and another nightmare of trying to preach and run a church while dreading that the telephone might ring at any time with bad news of Ann. Curiously enough it was in the weekend of greatest strain that I sat up in the middle of the night with the clear words in my mind that I should open my Bible at Dr. Moffat's translation of the 62nd Psalm. It was a Friday night at 3 a.m. when my fears for Ann in hospital were at their height. There I read the words which I had never read before since I had rarely used this particular translation of the Bible. "Leave it all quietly to God, my Soul". On the Sunday morning I took the words as my text and preached the only sermon in my life which before I left Rothesay a deputation of members asked me to repeat. Not only is it true that when you minister to others you minister to yourself, in preaching I discovered that the only way to preach is to preach to yourself.

Ann came home again in 1962 but this time to begin a period of years in which each few months it was possible to observe a deterioration in her exercise tolerance. For the last eight years of her life we both knew that there could only be one ending now. We both hoped and prayed that we might be spared a few good years together and we were. Among women I have seldom encountered a keener, more critical and intelligent mind than Ann possessed. As she came to have to spend more and more time in bed she took to reading 18th century history and a great deal of philosophy. We were still able to play chess together, to argue half the night about the philosophy of Wittgenstein or the theology of Bonhoeffer, most of all to read and re-assess our common interest in psychical research.

Here at this time I began to assess my ministry, and I came to see that again and again the greatest weakness of the orthodox church was that it had nothing to say to the basic hidden anxiety of most ordinary people. The problem of man's attitude towards death had become the principle evasion of the church. I found that again and again older people in particular confessed their hidden doubts and despair. Like the hungry sheep they looked up and were not fed.

Elisabeth Kubler-Ross, M.D., assistant Professor of Psychiatry at the University of Chicago has produced a remarkable study of attitudes to death and dying *On Death and Dying* (Tavistock Publications 1970). On the subject of the attitudes of clergy to the terminally ill patient she has this to say, "What amazed me, however, was the number of clergy who felt quite comfortable using a prayer book or a chapter out of the Bible as the sole communication between them and the patients, thus avoiding listening to their needs and being exposed to the questions they might be unable or unwilling to answer."

"Many of them had visited innumerable very sick people but began for the first time, in the seminar, really to deal with the question of death and dying. They were very occupied with funeral procedures and their role during and after the funeral but had great difficulties in actually dealing with the dying person himself."

It is also true that the author of the above also commends the sympathy and co-operation which she received from hospital chaplains but the fact remains that she has highlighted a problem which every clergyman feels, namely the embarrassment which the force of secular pressures has produced in clergy when dealing with the problem of death.

Just how serious is the lack of an open and uninhibited examination of such problems of despair is brought out by Prof. John Hinton in his book *Dying* (Penguin, 1967). He points out that in a report from North America there is revealed a noticeable rise in the number of deaths following the demise of wife or husband, especially among the younger people up to the mid-thirties. For widows the mortality rate rose to twice the normal for married women and for widowers of this age there was a fourfold increase at one stage after their wives' death. He also points out that in an English survey there was as much as a forty per cent increase in mortality rate in the first six months after bereavement in widowers. These figures deal only with mortality but what of the illness and incapacity which is the price our

24

society pays for its refusal to look squarely on the fact of death.

In the type of heart condition from which Ann suffered there are three possible terminations. Sudden cardiac arrest —the most merciful. Slow progressive failure until the patient is struggling for breath in bed and waterlogged by oedema or a severe embolism detaches from the heart and lodges in the brain. This may leave the unfortunate sufferer almost a vegetable, unable to move or speak. We lived for the last five years with this shadow on our lives together. You get used to anything. Ann to living in the knowledge that the end could come suddenly or otherwise. I to waking every few hours in the night and listening for the sound of Ann's breathing. But these last five years were the happiest of our lives. The more we each realised that any day could be the last, the more we found a quality of richness in being together.

I think the crowning blessing of the last few years when Ann's tolerance only allowed her to be out of bed for two or three hours each day, was the growing certainty of a sense of destiny which brought us together. In the marriages of some of my friends I find this developing quality over the years to be the most common indication of a happy marriage. "Wasn't it strange how we met," they say. When two people begin to look back over their lives together with a sense of awe and wonder at the "given-ness" of their relationship, an element of transcendence enters. This sense of a shared destiny is more common in marriages than often appears on the surface. It is sometimes only to a parish minister, perhaps at an anniversary that couples express this feeling.

In the summer of 1967 I received a call to Langside Old, a Glasgow parish. We both felt that there would be advantages in leaving, after eight years, the island of Bute. First in my mind was the fear that if Ann needed emergency treatment, such as sudden severe failure, then we would be better living in Glasgow. In spite of the idyllic beauty of living in a house on an island overlooking some of the most beautiful scenery in the world, there were other drawbacks. Ann was cut off from company a great deal. Her mother and two sisters lived on the mainland near Glasgow. My brother who was qualified in medicine and theology was minister in a Glasgow parish. It would mean that he could keep an eye on Ann's condition. We both had many friends in the area and we agreed that since I had to be out a great deal on parish business, the company of friends and relatives would be a good thing for Ann.

We left Bute and our friends on the island among which not the least were the amazing birds who attached themselves to us, including the thrush who wakened me every morning by coming in the bedroom window and landing on my head. While I dressed he walked up and down impatiently. Then he would walk along the pavement with me when I went for my morning newspaper and finally have his breakfast with us. Over three years he became as close to us as a dog might be. We couldn't look back at him as I drove off for the last time and left him sitting on the gate. Then there were the blue tits which came in and out as they pleased, sometimes spending most of the day in the kitchen. The robin who came in at 4 p.m. each afternoon during one winter and slept in my old tweed hat after an evening meal with us. People you can meet again or telephone but the birds we missed most of all, in Ann's case particularly, since they were her constant companions.

During the winter of 1967 when we came down to Glasgow Ann took her first severe infection for a number of years— bronchitis, the constant dread of heart patients. Again she had a long struggle and when she pulled through it, her degree of breathlessness was increased. It was heart-breaking to watch her pausing between each step in the house as she recovered her breath. The spring came, and I was able to take Ann out in a wheelchair, she had to give up all thought of walking outside now. Nevertheless, if she dressed slowly I could take her to a cinema, wheeling her into the stalls. This was one of the greatest of our pleasures in summertime, for in winter the risk of Ann getting an infection was too great. It was also possible in summer to take Ann in the car into fresh scenery and new places after being confined to the circuit of the island of Bute for so long.

During this time we were able to resume our interest in psychical research in a practical way. I met, in the home of one of my members, the medium whose evidence features so largely in this book, Albert Best. Once he became convinced that I was seriously interested, as a clergyman, in

26

his mediumship, he showed a willingness to demonstrate, particularly to any of my professional colleagues. On a number of occasions he held sittings in my home and my wife was present. I should make it clear that Ann had sat many times in the past with mediums, both alone and with me.

There is nothing even resembling the stage or cinema parodies of mediumship in the kind of "sitting" which Albert Best gave to us on four occasions in this period. Beyond knowing who I was and having tea with us later, we had no familiarity. Between these sittings I don't think I spoke to him except on the telephone when we arranged the dates. At such a "sitting" there would be present eight or ten people—often colleagues and their wives. My brother was present at some of these occasions. The company simply sat down in my lounge, not in a circle, but in any chairs they could find. It might be broad daylight in summer time as on two occasions, or normal electric lighting in winter as on the other occasions. All Albert Best required was silence for a few minutes while he went into a trance.

On the first "sitting" he named Bill, Ann's brother, and described him in detail. Bill named correctly the village in Belgium over which he had been shot down in 1944. Then he said to Ann, "Do you remember the old sewing machine at home where as a boy I used to keep my cigarette cards?" This was the kind of detailed memories which we were to get again and again in these "sittings". Of course Ann remembered, and then followed a string of memories. "Give my love to Daisy!" (Her mother's pet name in the family.) There must have been eighteen or twenty items in a short space, addressed to Ann. In each case the information was definite, precise and pertaining to the family background. Then came my turn. First my father was introduced to us carrying the biggest vegetable marrow I ever saw—as a joke I think. (My father's pride and joy was in growing vegetable marrows. He could never be satisfied and always hoped to produce larger ones.) This was the preliminary to my father describing three oil paintings which used to be in my boyhood home. Each painting he described in detail. For instance, there was a scene of Loch Ness and Castle Urquhart which had great sentimental value to me (my father speaking). My father had been born in Glen Urquhart.

I describe a typical "sitting" of the four such which we had with Albert Best. We knew that here was mediumship of a unique order. When I use the word "sitting" it is the usual term for an interview with a medium at which one, two or more people are present. One could just as readily call it a demonstration and indeed when mediumship is exercised in a large hall before an audience of hundreds the medium is normally called the demonstrator.

These four sittings with Albert Best meant a lot to Ann and myself for they produced some of the finest evidence for survival that we had received in recent years. Yet in all this time my wife only knew Albert Best formally and on both our parts the strictest precautions were taken that we would not convey any information. In a strange kind of way I had a feeling that the scene was being set and that the real drama was still to begin, as indeed it was.

Slowly and relentlessly Ann's tolerance to exercise of any kind deteriorated. We tried to have a short holiday by the sea together but it was a wild hope. In three days I had to rush Ann home by car again in failure. I knew that time was running out for us. September 1969 was our silver wedding and by an effort of will Ann managed to stay up for a few hours during the dinner in our home. She took her place beside me at the table and we celebrated what we both knew would be our last anniversary. We had never expected such a gracious gift as twenty-five years of life together when we married. Now we both felt that our bounty was complete.

Christmas and New Year came with a sense of foreboding on my part. Ann found it more difficult to sleep and had to be propped up on pillows. All this time she was bright and cheerful. On the last night of the year (31st December 1969) Ann had a curious premonitory dream, far more vivid than normal dreaming. The dream she described as preceded by a kind of click. She seemed to be half-awake in the dream, aware of being in her bedroom. Then the click and suddenly she was speaking to her father and her brother (both dead). They were smiling and light-hearted and Ann said to them, "How is it that I'm speaking to you when both of you are dead?" They continued to smile reassuringly and Bill, her brother, pointed to something in the room. Ann looked and saw that it was herself lying on the bed. Her father said, "It's as simple as that". Then followed the same 'click' sound and she awakened from her dream. In the morning Ann described her dream to me and we felt that it could mean just what it said, or rather, what they said.

On New Year's Day 1970 I took influenza but carried on without going to bed. Three days later Ann said, "I think my temperature is up a little". She always played down her physical symptoms. I had a sinking feeling in the pit of my stomach as I took her temperature; it was 103°. Sunday, Monday and Tuesday passed in a nightmare of swinging temperature and sickness in which I sat by her bedside day and night. Then on the Tuesday evening about 9 p.m. her temperature dropped and became normal and she asked for some light food. I made a milk pudding. "I feel quite good now," she said and her breathing became easier. An hour later she said, "I think I could sleep". I placed her pillows and tucked her in as usual and suddenly a quite unforgettable moment came. As I leaned over her she looked up into my eyes steadily.

Once again I had the same experience as on that Sunday morning many years ago. Tenderness is an inadequate word to describe the sudden transition when a relationship is experienced even for a few seconds, in a timeless quality. Again the shimmering, golden quality of light around Ann and vibrating in the room. We held on to that look. It was as though Ann was taking her last peaceful, calm look at me and I at her and all the time the tenderness, almost a visible thing between us. "You are my St. Francis and this is our Assissi," she said. Then, "We don't need words, do we?" she said, and smiled. I kissed her. "Go to sleep, darling!" I said, and she slept normally until 10 a.m. the following morning. These were the last free and significant words we were to exchange. The following morning at 10.30 a.m., half an hour after she awoke, the first blow came. At 10.30 a.m. her temperature was up again to 103° and still going up. This time her breathing was torture and the effort to cough constant.

The doctor advised immediate hospitalising. "And bring oxygen in the ambulance," he instructed over the telephone. My brother was with us and our own doctor. Later he confessed that as a medical man he thought she was going to die in the ambulance as we held the mask over her face.

However, she rallied and seemed a little more comfortable with constant oxygen in the ward. It was a virus bronchopneumonia. For the next forty-eight hours I hung about the ward. She was too weak to speak although she recognised me. My brother drove me to his place each night and I waited for the dreaded ringing of the telephone.

On the Saturday she seemed a little easier when I left her but her distress in breathing was very considerable. I meant to call again later that evening. An hour after I left her the telephone rang. Would I come in at once? I arrived and found her in great distress and hallucinating a little. Her breathing was more difficult and she had a sense of claustrophobia with the mask. I stood beside her bed holding the mask from 10 p.m. that evening until 10 a.m. the following morning. I think my presence helped her and made the receiving of oxygen easier for her. My brother insisted that I get a few hours sleep before I collapsed, as I still had the effects of my own influenza and hadn't been in bed for three nights now.

At 3 p.m. in the afternoon I saw her for a few minutes. She was too weak to speak and managed to wave her fingers and even smile as I left. "See you again in a couple of hours," I said.

Back at my brother's home I fell asleep in a chair. I suppose I would have slept for hours but the telephone rang and I heard someone answering. "Ann's condition has deteriorated, will you go in at once?" John, my brother, drove me to the hospital. We didn't speak much. As my twin brother he felt a great closeness to me in the ordeal. I ran up the stairs and was met by a nurse. "Come into the side room for a moment." "How is she?" I asked. "I'm afraid your wife died half an hour ago," she said. "We didn't want to break it to you over the telephone." "It was absolutely sudden—cardiac arrest, she just died in a second."

I didn't think to ask to see her. I just stood at the foot of her bed with the curtains drawn round it, in a daze. I went down the stairs and wished that they would stretch on for ever and never end.

My friend, Professor Murdo Ewan Macdonald, took the cremation service three days later. She had chosen the hymns for the service long ago. They were, "Oh Love That Wilt

Not Let Me Go" and at the end, "All Creatures of Our God and King, Lift up your voice and with us sing—Alleluia", St. Francis's "Hymn to the Sun", to be played *con vivace*.

Finally in her handbag I found written in her handwriting, the words of Elizabeth Barrett Browning. She must have copied them out in the evening when her influenza subsided.

> How do I love you? Let me count the ways,
> I love you to the depth, breadth and height my soul
> can reach.
> I love you to the level of every day's most quiet need
> —by sun and candlelight.
> I love you freely as men strive for right.
> I love you purely as they turn from praise.
> I love you with the passion put to use in my old
> griefs and with my childhood's faith.
> I love you with a love I seemed to lose with my lost
> saints.
> I love you with the breath, smiles, tears, of all my life
> And if God choose, I shall but love you better after
> death.

That piece of paper, and then silence and numbness and I was alone in a way in which I had never been alone before. My closest friends whom I loved became shadow creatures and their words had no meaning and it seemed that I, a shadowy figure, spoke to other shadowy figures. I continued to live with my brother for the next two weeks, since I had developed bronchitis. When this subsided I knew that I must be alone. I went back to live in the empty house. I sat on a chair in the empty bedroom. Cold January, and dark and alone with this sea of isolation surrounding me.

Suddenly I felt what I can only describe as a spark of light in the darkness within me and a sense of "being held". I found myself surprised as a child is surprised when it discovers that its fears are unfounded and that all is well. That was the mood as best I can describe it. It lasted only a few seconds, but its vividness remained. I felt eager to be back among the cares and problems of my parish and to reach out to other lives. I think I am open to life in a new kind of way and I believe that Ann is still part of me in an enduring and invulnerable way which I could never have imagined.

3

The first breaking of the silence took place on Monday 26th January—fifteen days after Ann died. I had been warned by some of my friends with experience of communication not to expect any clear evidence for at least three months or so. One of my friends, an eminent scientist with doctorates in Science and Philosophy, pointed out to me that there is a vast literature dealing with the technical problems of communications from the other side and that a period of adjustment would be necessary on the part of my wife. Also that my own grief and hers would create difficulties in communication. I did not therefore expect much when I arranged for my first sitting with Mrs. Findlater. Here is a transcript of that first sitting. I was a total stranger to this medium. The sitting was booked on the previous evening, by telephone. I gave my name, Mr. Kennedy, nothing more.

Mrs. Findlater went into light trance and a personality claiming to be a Burmese girl took over. This guide then appeared to act as intermediary. I shall simply call the guide by the medium's initials.

Mrs. Findlater: "There is a young man in Air Force uniform here. He was a rear-gunner, killed in action. He appears to know you very well. He throws his cap over your head in a gesture of familiarity.

"There are two fathers here, your father and your father-in-law. I feel that there was a passing about two weeks ago— your lady. She is here but she is still weak and in a period of resting. She finds it difficult to come close. Her body was utterly tired and used up. I feel complete exhaustion. She is being helped by your mother and the group around you. I feel that she knew about survival and communication. Spiritually she was much developed. There is a beautiful light around her. I feel that she will soon be bouncing back and making her presence felt. She just needs a little more rest.

"She is holding up a ring. Your mother is helping her to communicate. You gave her a ring, but there are two rings. You gave a ring to someone else. She is concerned about two other people on the earth plane. I see a ring like marcasite with a stone missing, it could be a brooch. I feel that she had something in her hand at her passing. She is holding up what looks like a testament. Did you put a testament in her hand before she passed over?" I answered "No". "Well, this is about the size of a testament, not square, but oblong. Yet it is not black or white but blue. Are there blue testaments? She insists that it was in her hand when she passed over." I replied that I could make no sense of this.

"She shows me curtains with one ring off at the top. Oh, the beautiful perfume. She was fond of perfume—not strong —but with a beautiful fragrance. She shows me what looks like a stick of perfume about $2\frac{1}{2}$ inches long, which she says she got in a present a few days before she passed over."

At this point the communication from my wife ceased. "She is tired at this point," said Mrs. F. My Mother took over. "Your mother says there was a wedding in the family recently." I agreed. " 'Yes,' says your mother, 'and my boy performed the ceremony'. The young couple are going to make a change, it will be good. Your brother has been bearing a cross of material worry recently. He has also had the cross of your bereavement to carry too. At present his faith is shaken and he wonders if there is anything to this whole business. He is not sure of his spiritual pilgrimage as you are. Your father also brings John Kennedy, also James and Alex.

"You do public speaking. You wear a dog-collar. Your wife returns with the help of your mother to say that she is very fond of hymns. I feel she liked to sing them. No, she is interrupting me to say, 'I never sang them, I always hummed them'." Here the sitting ended.

Let us examine the points brought out.

First, a young man in Air Force uniform, rear-gunner, killed in action. This is an exact description of my brother-in-law, Bill, killed in a bombing raid in 1944. He was a rear-gunner. He has communicated many times before, usually to give a message to his sister. This gesture of throwing his cap over my head he has also performed before. From a total stranger this is impressive. Two fathers here in spirit, father and father-in-law. This is accurate. Passing two weeks ago; accurate. Your lady; accurate. Still in period of resting, body utterly tired out and used up, complete exhaustion— again remarkably accurate. She is being helped by my mother. This is interesting in view of the fact that after a number of weeks this ceased to be necessary.

She knew about survival and communication—this is true. The remarks about the rings are true but not impressive since this could easily be guessed. The remark that she is concerned about two people is impressive, since she was greatly concerned about her mother and sister, for family reasons, just before she died and their situation also was still giving me concern. Ring or brooch with a stone missing. She had a silver pebble brooch with a stone missing which I gave to her sister. (Not too impressive, but fair.)

Now follows the most remarkable piece of evidence in the sitting. The remark about the testament which the medium felt was placed in her hand before she passed over. I would never dream of doing anything of this nature. Yet the medium insists that she had what she calls a testament —something oblong, blue, not black or white—in her hand when she passed over. A week later when I called at the hospital to pick up my wife's personal effects which were still awaiting collection, I noticed a bright blue plastic container of talcum powder on the top of the things in her large toilet bag. I was told that when she died suddenly of cardiac arrest she was still clutching this blue oblong container of talcum powder in her hand.

This is evidence of a highly persuasive nature since it is something I did not know. The medium did not know and if it was known to some nurse at the hospital, it was a detail, forgotten among the round of daily incidents and only revived in her memory at the sight of it again in my presence. Telepathy as an explanation of this kind of evidence is totally ruled out. This is one of the most forceful pieces of evidence I have received that I am in touch with the personality of my wife and that this memory at the instant of death has survived and is passed on to me as proof.

Curtains with a ring off at the top. True in the sense that she was always fussy about hooks coming off the curtains and many times sent me up on steps to remedy this. (Not strongly evidential, but fair and in character.)

The perfume remark could apply to almost any woman and is neutral as evidence.

The stick of perfume received in a present a few days before her passing. This is again good evidence. She received a porcelain handbag spray $2\frac{1}{2}$ inches long, with perfume, from a neighbour as a Christmas present 12 days before she died.

A wedding in the family—dead accurate. Three weeks earlier my niece was married and I performed the ceremony just as my mother stated.

The remarks about my brother's material worry are not in themselves evidence of survival but they are completely accurate. The remarks regarding his loss of faith are also accurate. He is qualified in theology and medicine and had just recently resigned from his church to return to medical practice. The names: John Kennedy, my grandfather on my father's side of the family, James and Alec were the names of two of my uncles on my father's side. I do public speaking, wear a dog collar. This information might have been available to the medium.

Finally, my wife was very fond of hymns and used to sing them to me when I came home from church after she had heard them on television programmes while in bed. Yet it was the interruption, "I never sang, I always hummed them" which so impressed me. On reflection I realised that she hardly ever sang the words of a song in her life. She always hummed. The very nature of this as an interruption and correction is impressive.

So much for the first sitting with Mrs. Findlater to whom I was a total stranger, fifteen days after my wife died. The blue testament which turned out to be a plastic talcum powder container. The stick of perfume. The knowledge in such dramatic form that she hummed and did not sing. These are first class items of evidence. The other items such as description of the illness, short time passed over, are good but second class evidence in the sense that assuming telepathy to be something more vast and inclusive and accurate than it has ever been demonstrated to be under laboratory conditions, then this could be an explanation.

It is important to remember that I approached Mrs. Findlater as a total stranger and that she lives in a town 40 miles away from Glasgow and arrived that morning for my sitting at one of the well-known Spiritualist churches. I made the booking in the usual way as an enquirer. I must also point out that a considerable integrity in relation to private sittings with mediums is the rule among most S.N.U. churches. It is indeed a point of honour never to reveal any information about a sitter to a visiting medium. I am satisfied as to the honesty and integrity of everyone concerned with this sitting.

The next break in the silence took place sixteen days later on the 12th February. This piece of evidence concerns a medium whom I had come to know fairly well over the last two years. He attended my wife's funeral and had given sittings four times to a group in my home during the previous summer and winter. Therefore he knew my wife slightly, although he had never been alone with her. He had met her in the company of others. As the mediumship of Mr. Albert Best will figure largely in this section of the book, this is perhaps the time to give something of his background.

Mr. Best was born in Belfast, served in North Africa during the last war, was wounded and discharged, became a postman in the Ayrshire town of Irvine and continued for 20 years as a postman. He was aware of psychic happenings even as a child, when he spoke of seeing persons when others were unaware of anyone present. Before I met Albert Best two years ago, he had retired from the Postal Service after twenty years' service and, at the age of fifty had come to live in Glasgow. He has healing gifts and is growing in reputation both as healer and medium in Spiritualist circles. Albert Best is the person who has provided some of the most convincing evidence in this narrative. Nevertheless, while I respect his honesty and sincerity, the reader should be aware that I know him as a personal friend. My wife had only met him on four occasions socially and at no time had any long or intimate conversation with him.

On Thursday, 16th February, I was entertaining a young married couple to dinner in my flat when the telephone rang. This was Albert Best on the other end, "Have you been opening wine or spilt some wine? Your wife came through a few minutes ago and asked me to get in touch with you. She says that she was beside you when you took out a new tablecover, lace or embroidered, something about a new wine."

Comment. An hour earlier I had decided to put an embroidered tablecover on the dining table, which I did. I had just opened a bottle of a new type of wine which I had never sampled before.

At this same conversation on the telephone Albert Best said, "One last impression from your wife, does the name, Scott, mean anything to you?" This reference to the name, Scott, is interesting and will appear later.

My comment on the above is that it is not particularly convincing evidence in itself. Nevertheless, one must face the possibility that if the survival hypothesis is true, then most of the communications which we receive will be of an emotional and personal nature. In other words, if you could grab a telephone and blurt out a few words on a very bad line to someone at the other end of the world, or if there existed the possibility of a few seconds communication with a loved one beyond the barrier of death, most of us would simply blurt out—"It's me! I love you, darling, don't be unhappy, carry on, I'm always near you."

Particularly in the emotional period of greatest grief just after a bereavement, we must accept the possibility that if we survive death, our loved ones are just as much choking with emotion as we are. In fact during one of my later and finest sittings with the London medium, Mrs. Ena Twigg, I found that the sense of my wife's presence and personality was so strong that tears were running down my cheeks and I was almost unable to reply to questions. Surely it is not unreasonable that our loved ones may approach that communication with the same emotional difficulties. Hence the triteness of what comes through so often and its lack of value as evidence to the non-involved critic.

The next incident took place on the 18th February when I had booked my second sitting with Mrs. Findlater. "Your lady is here, she is still progressing, still a little weak and has a long way to go. When she is speaking she gesticulates a great deal, using her hands like this." (At this point the medium placed her hands in a replica of a favourite gesture of my wife's which was typical of her when excited.) "She says something in what seems to me like Italian, a word like 'funicula'. She says you put her ring into a pocket book before you came here." (This was true, I had transferred her wedding ring from a drawer in my bureau to my pocket book with the intention of taking it to a jeweller's and suggesting that it might be altered for my fingers.)

"She is worried about her mother on earth, who is grieving too much." (This again was true, I had been involved in trying to comfort my mother-in-law during the week as she had been having bouts of weeping and depression.)

"Your mother is here and also your father. There was a deep understanding between you and your mother. She says you studied Divinity but you could have done medicine and would like to have studied law." (This again is absolutely accurate.) "Your mother shows me a cameo brooch, it was a gift from your father because she looks towards him as she shows it to me." (This again is interesting as I could not remember a cameo brooch. However, on looking through some old photographs I came on one of my father and mother shortly after they were married. My mother is wearing a brooch and on examining it through a magnifying glass it is clearly a cameo brooch.)

"Your wife is in the background all the time but she still finds difficulty in communicating. She shows me a cocktail dress, the colour is shimmering green or blue. Your wife painted in oils, she is showing me paintings, your mother is helping her to get close. Your wife was very fond of paintings. She is showing me some in your home. Also there was one of hers which is not finished." (At this point my wife seemed to be exhausted with the effort and faded.)

"Your mother is here with Aunt Kate. She says that they didn't get on too well when they were on the earth plane but they co-operate a great deal here. She says that you went into a dressing table and took something out and looked at it and put it back the other day." (A small piece of evidence. I did take a Valentine card out of a dressing table drawer and put it back. It is also perfectly true that my mother and her sister, Kate, were constantly quarrelling and "not speaking" as I remember them in my childhood.) Here the sitting ended.

My comment on the above is that there is nothing of

first class evidential value. Yet the remarks are accurate and consistent. To the critic there is nothing which might not be explained on the extended telepathy theory. Namely, that the human psyche contains powers to dip deep into the unconscious memories of the sitter at such an interview. One rather interesting thing was that during the sitting while the purported guide of the medium was giving a rather lengthy moral uplift talk—the kind of padding which is part of so many sittings—my mother interrupted, i.e. the guide stopped and said, "Your mother is annoyed with me for wasting time, she says we have only a short time, let's get on with the evidence."

Now this impatience was totally characteristic of my mother and also the forthrightness which would be capable of interrupting if necessary. This means that the medium seems to be capable of conveying a dramatic quality which is totally consistent with the personality of my mother as I remember her. Notice also that the same medium puts her hands and fingers into a characteristic gesture of my wife's which I doubt if I have seen any other woman use.

This means that a very impressive part of the evidence for the presence of an invisible personality cannot always be conveyed in a verbal report of dialogue. There are qualities of gesture, impatience, confidence, reticence, which may be conveyed by a medium at a sitting which is totally absent from a written account of what took place but which goes a long way to creating the strong impression that one is in the presence of a remembered personality.

It is true my wife painted in oils and it is also true that one of her last efforts at dressmaking was a shimmering green cocktail dress which she did not have the strength to finish. There was an unfinished oil painting in a large folio in which my wife kept her painting materials and which I had left unopened since her death, so I was not aware of this.

The placing by Mrs. Findlater of her fingers in a characteristic gesture was done with all the imitative sense of someone looking at another person and attempting to convey a picture. This was most interesting.

4

At this point it is possible to gain the impression that following my wife's death my life was one long succession of visits to various mediums for solace. This was not so. During the time of which I am writing I was carrying out my pastoral duties in a busy city parish. Visting in hospitals, conducting funerals and officiating at weddings, in addition to visiting my parishioners in their homes and conducting two services of public worship on a Sunday which meant writing two sermons each week, at least.

All this time I believed that Ann survived, that she was going through the inevitable after-death period of resting and recuperation, more especially in her case, since she had been an invalid, only able to be outside in a wheel-chair for the last two years.

It is true that there were low periods when I forgot the strength of the evidence I had read and experienced in the past. During these low periods I would find myself beginning to doubt the validity of all my reading and experience in investigating the question of survival. Sometimes I wondered, sometimes the silence became an overwhelming emptiness and loss. Sometimes I wept—tears of self-pity, no doubt— but all part of the normal human reaction when we are low and our emotions take over from our intellect. I hoped to put myself in the position of an investigator, drawn to find out about survival after the loss of a loved one. At least I would know to what extent grief and loss and emotional involvement affected the evidence.

At the beginning of March I booked a sitting with a medium with whom I had had no previous contact. After over half an hour of sitting and listening to a description of spirit-guides and helpers, all of whom were new to me, I left the sitting without any mention of Ann. No message, no evidence. The mere report that I had a mother on the other side, which at my age seemed a fairly even-money bet.

Yet to be fair, this woman did give the name and describe a minister who had come through at a sitting a year previously.

At the close of the sitting she mentioned two names of people who wanted to come through and gave their names. The first was Gavin Maxwell, the well known author of *Ring of Bright Water,* etc., who had died a few months previously and whom I had never met. The second name was Graham Moffat, author of *Bunty Pulls the Strings,* at one time a well known Scottish playwright and dead these many years. So ended a sitting which appeared to lean to the fantastic. Except that the following day I was lunching with a friend and played over to him the tape of this abortive sitting since I valued his opinion. When we came to the Gavin Maxwell part he sat up. "Gavin Maxwell was my friend, and we co-operated in a shark hunting venture." The short message he found interesting and exciting.

Almost ten weeks later I was having dinner with Maurice Barbannell, editor of *Psychic News,* when in the course of talking about the stalwarts in the cause of spiritualism in the past he spoke of Graham Moffat, author of *Bunty Pulls the Strings,* one of the most brilliant speakers in the cause of spiritualism of his time.

Finally, in this sitting the name, Scott, is repeated twice. "Of the Antarctic," I quipped, jokingly. "No, in a book you have been reading," was the reply. "Read up to chapter 5 again and don't skip so much."

Now it was perfectly true that I had been reading a book by a woman, Jane Sherwood, called *Post Mortem Journal* in which there is claimed to be an account obtained by automatic writing of a communicator who calls himself Scott and who purported to be Lawrence of Arabia describing his reactions from the time of his sudden death in the motor cycle crash and his becoming aware that he survived on the other side. I had been reading the book with some scepticism, since one naturally doubts the authenticity of communications from so-called celebrities. Nevertheless, for the second time, first with Albert Best, the name Scott appears.

On the 5th March I was having dinner with Albert Best. We did not mention mediumship, indeed I think we spoke of football and chatted generally. Although I could have asked Albert Best to try to concentrate his mediumistic ability on getting some kind of evidence, I always felt that was too much like "singing for one's supper". I also felt that since we were personal friends, it would put him in an invidious position if he simply felt nothing. Albert Best, to his credit, said to me at this time, "You realise that I feel no sense of your wife's presence. When I think of her I just get nothing, so there it is." This impressed me as a particularly honest reaction. It would have been simple for the imposter to have invented a few non-committal sentences.

Nevertheless, at the end of the meal Albert Best said, "I feel that Ann is very faintly trying to get through. She appears to be trying to give you evidence of something of which you are not aware. I see a slim box-like thing made of wood or plastic, roughly 4 inches square. It has a mosaic of colours in light brown and yellow. I think it is used for holding matches, the kind of thing which would hold two boxes of Swan Vestas. This is not in your home, but make enquiries about it because I feel that it is simply given as a piece of evidence in which you will have to do detective work and rule out the possibility of telepathy." A week later I discovered that a cousin and close friend of Ann had exactly such a match box holder on her table and I had not been in her home since my wife's death. The description was accurate. Trivial perhaps? But the best of evidence is usually trivial.

So far the communications or alleged communications from Ann have been sporadic and not often of the best evidential value. With certain exceptions. The remarkable first sitting two weeks after her passing. Then it was claimed that she was really relaying the evidence through my mother.

When Ann attempts to communicate herself, there is always difficulty. The medium usually finds that words are difficult to convey. The remark, "Try to come closer" is often made. It does appear that in the period immediately after death there is a barrier of emotion and grief on both sides. A recently passed communicator is often described as overcome with emotion and to be truthful for the first few months I found tears in my eyes and a lump in my throat also. It is only after almost three months that the phase which I would describe as producing satisfactory evidence begins. The ideal conditions for communications are calmness, a little light-heartedness to be capable of laughing together at a remembered joke also helps. In other words, "naturalness" is the key to the best evidence and the finest communication.

This is literally impossible in the first few months after a bereavement. I knew this in theory, but I had to experience it in my own case to really appreciate how true it is. From about mid-March the quality of Ann's own evidence begins to improve and more and more I am aware of the same lively, intelligent personality producing the kind of evidence which we had agreed we would try to do.

On Sunday, the 15th March, there occurred one of the really remarkable incidents which seem to indicate the concern and awareness which our loved ones have for us from the other side. Sunday 15th March was my Communion Sunday and in the Church of Scotland Communion or the Sacrament of the Lord's Supper is only celebrated twice or three times a year in most churches. It can mean two long and exhausting services, each lasting for $1\frac{1}{2}$ hours with interviews between each service and a hasty snack in the church. One may arrive at the church at 10 .m. and return home at 4 p.m. literally exhausted and depleted of nervous energy.

Normally, when my wife was alive, I would stretch out on the sofa and sleep deeply in total exhaustion for an hour and a half. Then about 5.30 p.m. Ann would come through from the bedroom and awaken me in preparation for going out at 6 p.m. for my evening service.

On this particular Sunday, March 15th, I came home as usual at 4 p.m. exhausted. Rather foolishly I lay down on the sofa and in minutes I was deeply asleep. So deeply asleep that I am certain I would have slept for hours blissfully removed from the prospect of an evening congregation assembled and no minister arriving to conduct the service. I was deeply asleep. Gradually I became aware of the intrusion of a bell continuing to ring. The ringing continued and I slowly awakened to the fact that the telephone was ringing.

I staggered from the sofa, still half-asleep, picked up the telephone and heard a woman's voice say, "Is that the Reverend David Kennedy? My name is Mrs. Lexie Findlater. I am telephoning from Grangemouth (a town 40 miles away). Your wife is impressing me so strongly that I have to telephone you now. I have tried to write a letter and put off this feeling but I am being told that I must telephone you now, now, she is so insistent, yet I have no idea why. Your wife is simply saying, 'Get out now and use the old notes'. I don't know what it means but I had to do this."

Now Mrs. Findlater, it will be remembered, was the medium whom I had met in the two private interviews described earlier, the first one two weeks after my wife's death. She only knew my name and not my address. She had to find my address and telephone number from directory enquiry. It took amazing confidence and courage to telephone a person who was almost a total stranger and then say that she did not know why she was telephoning except that my wife was impressing her that she had to do this.

I thanked Mrs. Findlater for telephoning and explained to her that if she had not telephoned me at this moment I would have slept right through the time of my evening service—it was 6 p.m. when she telephoned. I had just time to grab the notes of an old sermon, rush into my car and arrive at the church, get into my robes and 'make it' for 6.30 p.m. evening service.

Now here is a case where my wife claimed that she saw me sleeping deeply, likely to miss my evening service. It was her habit to awaken me. There was only one way to get me to my church in time. She could not herself impress me, so she impressed strongly a more sensitive person, this woman 40 miles away, and got the thought across that she must telephone me. In other words, Ann managed to do for me what she had always done, awaken me on this particular Sunday. I had always relied on her to do this. If there is a better example of loving concern and intervention from our dear ones on the other side, it would be difficult to find.

Yet this is not the end. Three days later Albert Best telephoned me and after an amazing message from my wife, concluded by saying, "And Ann says, 'For heaven's sake get an alarm clock and don't sleep in again at the end of the week'."

Now comes the amazing evidence of that telephone call from Albert Best. Before the telephone rang I was in the middle of the kind of job a man has to learn to do for himself when he is living alone. I decided that my yellow pullover was in need of washing. I knew the general rules about washing woollens carefully and gently in warm water and soap flakes. I'm afraid I was over indulgent with the soap flakes. Anyhow, in a short time I had the basin overflowing with soap suds in a rich lather while I squeezed away at my yellow pullover.

Just then the telephone rang. Albert Best on the other end. "Are you shampooing, I mean not your hair, something woollen? I see lather, suds overflowing and something woollen in the basin. Your wife is saying that she was watching you doing this." I told Albert that I was actually washing a pullover in soap suds when he interrupted me. He replied, "Well, your wife is saying, 'Put in the black pullover while you are at it, the one with the egg stains on it, it needs washing badly'." Then followed the remark about getting an alarm clock which I have already referred to. Needless to say there was a black pullover, with egg stains, which I had forgotten about and which badly needed washing.

What does one make of this? Is it a fantastic form of telepathy in which an ordinary ex-postman has powers which would make him a fortune on stage or television? In which he knows not only exactly what I am doing, but the contents of my linen cupboard? Or is it the more reasonable explanation that my wife, who was always fussy about my dress and appearance and also insisted on doing these washing jobs right to the end, is still close and still aware and still concerned and because of the unique situation of my being in touch with a gifted medium, is able to show that same concern from beyond the barrier of death?

It is important to realise that only in very rare instances is this kind of communication or communion in any sense a conversation. In some cases the medium sees an inward picture of the person communicating from the other side. Thus he may describe features. He may at the same time be shown symbols and hear words or even brief sentences. This may come to him in semi-trance or deep trance and control by a guide. It is difficult to be sure on some occasions whether the guide is a separate entity or secondary personality of the medium. However, the idea of guides in the spirit world should not be foreign to orthodox church people, for the Ministry of Angels or Guides and the Greek word 'angelos' which simply means a 'messenger' is one of the comforting doctrines which has not been emphasised enough in recent centuries, but it is perfectly orthodox.

To the critic who says, "Why don't the dead speak up more clearly, why all the signs and symbols and brief phrases?" The perfectly reasonable answer is that communication involves a change of normal conditions for the communicator on the other side as well as a change of normal conditions for the medium on this side. In addition, the thoughts and emotions of the "sitter" are impinging on the part of the mind of the medium which is sensitive to impressions. Communicators have described it as like trying to speak on a poor telephone connection to a stenographer who is deaf and almost unable to concentrate. The wonder is that good and impressive evidence is obtained at all.

Here, bearing in mind these difficulties, is a remarkable communication of 19th March. My wife is improving in the art, if we can so call it, of communication. Albert Best telephoned. "Your wife is trying to get a message through, I have a strong impression of her beside me while writing a letter. She is referring to something which happened in connection with her young brother, Bill, (who was killed as an air-gunner in 1944). Something which happened in the days before the war when they were all at home. This is a joke in the family in relation to milk, either going for milk or something about milk in relation to Bill. You don't know about it but you will be able to find out. There was also a blue ribbon originally wrapped round an Easter egg —I feel it is a childhood memory which you will be able to check up on at her home. You know nothing about either and she is giving this as evidence. She also speaks about 'cuff links'."

I visited Ann's mother and younger sister. Her mother is seventy four and her memory is not always perfect. At first there was no response to the question I asked, "Was there any joke in the family which Ann would know about concerning her brother Bill and relating to milk?" It seemed to be a blank. Then, during tea, my mother-in-law suddenly remembered and her face lit up. When her son Bill was sixteen years of age, he had a beautiful thick crop

47

of wavy auburn hair. As boys will do, he could not afford expensive hair cream and one summer he hit on the idea of applying milk to his hair, as a dressing. This he did for a fortnight or so until gradually the milk became rancid and the smell in the room when Bill came in became a source of embarrassment. Eventually the smell was traced to Bill's hair and the truth came out that Bill had been applying milk as a hair dressing for weeks. For months afterwards it was a family joke, much to the embarrassment of Bill. Remember the words of Albert Best, "There was a joke in the family about Bill, Ann's young brother, concerning milk."

Surely this is beyond coincidence or one might ask in how many families could a similar joke have applied and similar events have taken place? I have never heard of a similar story in my life. The message was categorical. The conclusion seems to be that either Albert Best has the power to tap the forgotten memories of anyone at will and tag them on to a dramatic sense of my wife's personality and be deluded himself by the picture of my wife's presence which appears to him while receiving the message, or the personality or some part of the personality and memories of my wife, Ann, has survived the change we call death and is making an effort to produce evidence of survival to me and also to produce the kind of evidence which we both agreed before she died would be regarded as compelling evidence of survival.

To the question, whose anniversary is 21st March, I have found no answer yet.

The reference to blue ribbon round an Easter egg which she kept as a child, I must disregard as good evidence because, although my mother-in-law seems to remember this, it is the kind of thing that almost any girl would do and is weak as evidence.

5

About the middle of April came two of the finest pieces of evidence of all. Each item is distinct and precise. Both were given to me by Albert Best over the telephone. The usual procedure is that Mr. Best may be doing anything, writing a letter, making a meal, when suddenly he is aware of my wife. He claims to see her in an inward sense and hear her words. This time I was told, "Your wife is here again, she keeps setting me puzzles. She is saying something about ballet shoes. She tells me that you don't know about them, but if you will ask at home you will discover. She is laughing. It seems to be a joke about ballet shoes." Apart from the fact that when Ann was fit she liked to go to ballet. I knew of no connection with ballet shoes.

Oddly enough about twenty minutes after Albert's call, Ann's youngest sister telephoned me about some trivial matter. As she said in conversation she just took a notion to telephone me. At that time I hadn't heard from her for weeks. I took the opportunity of putting my questions to her carefully. I asked, "Would ballet shoes have any significance in relation to Ann? Was there ever a joke in the family in relation to ballet shoes which concerned Ann?" Mary, Ann's sister paused for a few seconds. I felt the silence of someone obviously startled, even over the telephone. She replied, "This is really odd, only Ann and I knew of an incident which we treated as a private joke. It concerned ballet shoes and took place twenty-five years ago, shortly after you were married.

"Ann came to visit us. There was nobody in the house. She opened the door, came in and saw on the dresser a pair of ballet shoes which I had just got, when as a girl of fourteen at this time, I started my first lessons. Ann was intrigued by them.

"On a whim she decided to put them on and try pointing her toes. Of course the shoes were too small and she could keep them on her feet only by holding the ribbons in her hands.

"Suddenly I came in. There she was in the centre of the room trying to hold on my ballet shoes, pointing her toes and looking ridiculous. We both laughed. It remained a private joke between us."

Here is something totally unknown to me. Something which took place twenty-five years ago. Only known to two persons, my wife and her young sister and long forgotten by that sister but brought to mind again by my question about a joke in relation to ballet shoes. The force of this remarkable evidence is not even exhausted yet, for in a later telephone call, Albert Best, a few days later relays from my wife, "You got the telephone call. Yes, I impressed her to call you." "I don't know who she's talking about," said Mr. Best. So this carefully thought out and succinctly tailored piece of evidence seems to me to be one of the finest examples of a directing intelligence producing evidence unknown to me and at the same time impressing the person who has the key to the evidence to telephone me. Both fit together and I am left marvelling at the quality of this evidence, as one marvels at a line of poetry.

I began very early in this quest to ask myself, did it really happen. So much so that from the second week after Ann's death I kept a large diary and noted the exact words of each incident, noting also the time of day and date. Even as I write the account of this, a month after the event, having first of all written it up carefully in my diary when it happened, I am aware of hardly being able to keep pace with the evidence. Today I took a patient who is crippled by arthritis in my car to the healing sanctuary where Albert Best does three or four sessions each week.

He suddenly turns aside from laying his hands on a patient to say to me, "Your wife says you telephoned Kilmarnock." I agreed that I had telephoned someone in Kilmarnock yesterday. "Yes, it was the Gemmells," replied Albert, "and you have been cleaning your windows and you did something to the hem of curtains and finally your wife says you came out today and forgot your handkerchief." All of which was absolutely true. I did help my cleaner to pin up the hem of curtains which she washed two days ago. I did clean the windows two days ago and for the first day in years I had come out without a handkerchief. Albert concludes it all with a smile, "Just to let you know how close to you your wife is."

This is mediumship of a particularly brilliant kind. What Albert Best does in providing proof for me he also does for many others. The only difference is that in my case I have carefully recorded and dated the evidence. Others receive this kind of evidence, perhaps not as often nor with the same high quality of directing intelligence behind it. But in many cases the wonder of the evidence is forgotten after a few days and the details obscure in a week or two.

The curious thing about evidence of survival is that the best evidence of mental mediumship is not contained in the long narrative descriptions or long messages from the other side. During the months following Ann's death I booked sittings with a number of mediums who gave me messages claimed to be from Ann. Some of them may have been genuine. It may be that Ann took time off from serious, carefully thought out evidence to relax in descriptions of the other side.

Ann sometimes spoke of the glorious colours; the indescribable music; her continued interest in painting; the fact that she was aware of higher beings, 'Shining Ones' as she called them. But the fact is that all these descriptions have little or no evidential value. By their nature they are non-verifiable. A great deal of the books produced by automatic writing are in this category. They mostly carry a certain consistency but it would appear that it is as difficult to describe the dimension into which we pass after death, as it is to describe this three dimensional world which we inhabit in our five senses.

I have just had a visit from a neighbour who has been to the Channel Islands. All he describes to me are the gardens he saw, the roses, the quality of the soil. If I were to take his impression, Jersey is one vast garden. I suppose someone else might describe it as a vast amusement arcade. To someone else it would appear to be endless beaches and sunshine.

How could a surviving personality describe the dimension into which he enters? Certainly only in terms of reference which would be meaningful to us. But this is one phase of communication which we will have to leave to each imagination.

The other thing is, personal emotion, endearments, affection. By its very nature communications from the other side contain phrases like "she is overcome with emotion", "She just cannot describe what it means to her to have this opportunity to say that she is still the same, that she will always love you," "My darling. I'll never leave you and our love will always be," "Whatever happens we will still have each other".

Such sentences may be coloured by the vocabulary of the medium, I believe this to be so. They can never be evidence of survival. Yet if they come as they do, in the midst of serious, verifiable evidence of survival, there is a compelling power, a loveliness and a heart to heart simplicity about them. They ring true. True to Ann as I knew her and true to our relationship. They come, these openings of the floodgates of affection and I accept them and respond for we cannot always be engaged in producing evidence. Even two scientists, husband and wife, may spend the day in cold assessment of lines of precipitation but in the evening there is time to make the non-scientific assertion. "I love you".

On Thursday, 9th April, in my own home I had arranged a sitting with Mrs. Findlater, largely for the benefit of two members of my church who were keenly interested in the problem of survival and communication. The sitting opened with Mrs. Findlater being controlled by her guide, the Burmese girl. The first person to come through was a Tibetan Lama who claimed to have been with me for a long time. He even gave his name, Zepala. Anyone contacting Spiritualism for the first time will soon become aware of the claim that evil people attract evil entities. Most ordinary persons and especially persons aspiring to moral qualities and trying to express love and concern in their lives, such people it is claimed are assigned guides in the dimension we call the Spirit World for lack of a better name. Now the concept of guides is not an unorthodox one from the Christian point of view.

Indeed the Archbishops of York and Canterbury's commission which enquired into Spiritualism in 1937 in its majority report which was never officially published, makes the observation, "The belief in guardian angels or guides has been very general in Christianity". There is nothing inherently foolish or contradictory from the Christian viewpoint in the concept of guides. It is claimed that these guides (and two or three depending on the range of a person's activities in his spiritual pilgrimage) help us by inspiring us and preparing the way for us. Much that we would call providence, it is claimed, is the direct result of guides helping us and many of our ideas, thoughts and inspirations come from such guides.

I can only say that I find nothing inherently foolish or nonsensical about this. I have said that we attract entities in harmony with our own personality. If a person is vain and foolish and ignorant he will attract vain, mischievous and foolish entities who will claim to be persons like Cleopatra, Nefertiti, Julius Caesar and Napoleon. Whether these entities are facets of the foolish sitter's personality or separate spirit beings having a lark, we cannot at present tell.

Regarding the question of Spirit Guides the New Testament has some interesting light to throw on the subject.

In St. Matthew's Gospel, chapter 18, verse 10, there occurs a saying of Jesus which has largely been ignored by clerics. In referring to little children, Jesus says "Their angels do always behold the face of my father which is in heaven".

What does this mean? It has been widely held among spiritualists that even from birth, guides are given the task of inspiring and protecting each human soul in its journey through life. That many of the names they give or identities they claim are on the face of it ridiculous, I do not deny. But this only applies to a limited number of so-called guides. Many of these entities appear to be personalities who have lived on earth at some period. Their influence appears to be entirely beneficent and concerned in helping us in our spiritual growth.

The other explanation of such entities claiming separate existence and often having access to information not available to the conscious personality, is that they are part of the phenomena of multiple personality. Human personality may be so complex as to include such phenomena beyond the level of normal consciousness.

When Jesus speaks of angels (or in its Greek form "messengers") is this a licence for believing in Spirit Guides? The most modern of Gospel commentaries, the Penguin

Commentary by J. C. Fenton, has this to say on the passage I have quoted, "Everyone has his heavenly representative, an angel who guards him and prays to God for him" (page 245). One of the most definitive studies of the subject of Angels is the writer of the article on Angels in Hastings' *Dictionary Of Christ and the Gospels*". He holds that Christians are bound to accept the "prima facie" New Testament teaching as to the angelic ministry. The article gives no fewer than ten examples in which it is clear that Jesus believed in the existence and ministry of angels. Thus it is impossible to argue that an isolated example might be the result of an addition by some over-enthusiastic later editor. We just cannot escape from the overwhelming evidence that the teaching of Jesus is categorical in stating that angels do exist and that they do help and inspire us.

It seems reasonable to ask the question today; is the expression spirit guide not simply a modern translation of angel, which as I have pointed out in the original Greek manuscripts simply means "messenger". I cannot see how the Christian can escape from accepting the existence of higher entities or guides who are attached to us and help us. So for me there is no contradiction in accepting the existence of spirit guides at its best and the teaching of Jesus regarding the ministry of angels.

This is one good reason why the case for spirit guides cannot be airily dismissed. There are numerous other examples of guides helping to produce evidence such as in the case of the Rosemary scripts.

I am not prepared to dismiss the assertion that I have a guide on the basis of the worst of spiritualist tomfoolery. We must judge guides by their best and highest examples and I recommend anyone to read the teachings of Silver Birch to judge such spirit guides at their best.

To revert to my sitting. A Tibetan Lama, Zepala comes forward, admires the soapstone Buddha on my mantleshelf and mentions that I have a smaller one in a drawer in my bureau. He refers to a curious phenomenon which I had noticed before, that my handwriting changes suddenly from its normal bold lettering to a spidery script at times. This is true, it had puzzled me before. "This is when we try to take over and inspire you".

At this point Ann comes through. She is happy that I am

coming to accept the loss of her physical presence, but I shall be more and more aware of her spiritual presence.

Now Ann begins to describe my previous church at Rothesay on the Island of Bute. You go up a small avenue to the main door, but there is a side door which she used. She sat on the second seat or pew on the side where nobody else sat. Absolutely true.

She has been in my next church. (I had moved to Langside in Glasgow, a large city parish, two and a half years ago, and the seat where she sat is always vacant.) Now my mother intervenes. She is holding up her left hand (a gesture she has made before when coming through different mediums in the last ten years). She apparently does this to remind me that when she was dying I held her left hand until the end. She suffered from a stroke.

My father comes, gives his name, David, and begins to speak about my twin brother. (This is very natural as John, my twin brother, and my father were very close.) John is worried about a partnership problem just now. This is totally accurate, he was withdrawing from the medical partnership where he practised at this time. Nobody knew this except my brother and his family and myself. Father tells me to tell John not to worry too much, another gate is about to open. A week later John received an offer to join another partnership which he found more congenial. A word of encouragement followed from my father to the younger of the two ladies in John's home. This I take to be his seventeen year old daughter. She is urged to dig her heels in and study. At the time she was finding it rather a strain studying for her "highers".

Ann returns again and refers to a three-strand pearl necklace which I gave to someone recently. I had just given her sister a three-strand pearl necklace two days earlier. Ann concludes by saying the words, "There is a land of pure delight. I was there, you know." On the previous Sunday evening I had decided to introduce a hymn which my congregation had not sung before in my time, "There is a land of pure delight". Ann finally said that she was getting through a little easier now and she was delighted to come through in her own home. She was becoming stronger and progressing. She still felt a little of the sense that she ought to be breathless after so many years of this condition. "But I am getting better and better."

Finally, as she said goodbye, she finished, "And change the flowers in the crystal vase". This referred to flowers in a crystal vase beside her photograph in my bedroom which was locked and which the medium had no opportunity to see. Here the sitting ended.

Not a tremendously evidential sitting from my point of view. The reference to the hymn was correct. The description of my Rothesay Church and the place where she sat was dead accurate. The fact that her seat in my new church was empty and no one sat near her, was also accurate.

My father's message to John my brother was totally accurate and described in detail his personal problems. (Of how many persons would it be true to say that they had partnership problems and not to worry, another gate would open?)

The other sitters, Mr. G. and his wife, were told some remarkable things by this medium. She gave a name, John Wood, and this communicator referred to the fact that Mr. G. was wearing his pullover. It was a fact that this was the name of a close friend of Mr. G. and when he died three years ago his widow asked Mr. G. to accept and wear two of her husband's golfing pullovers in his memory and my friend was wearing one, the yellow pullover, at the sitting.

On this basis one has to consider that Mrs. Findlater, whatever she may be, has remarkable powers. This is not the type of evidence which is unknown to the sitters, but it carries a great deal of weight when it is repeated and repeated again and again. All the time against the background of the claim that our friends and loved ones beyond the veil are chatting or attempting to chat by odd words and symbols and trying to convince us of their presence.

6

Some months previously I had accepted an invitation to be present at the *Psychic News and Two Worlds* dinner in London. At the same time I agreed to speak at a number of Spiritualist propaganda meetings at which Albert Best was to demonstrate platform clairvoyance. These were mostly in London with the exception of one meeting at Ipswich.

As I was due a week's holiday from my pastoral duties at Langside, I decided that it would be better for me to be fully occupied, rather than being the sole occupant of some coast hotel in the month of April. So on the 23rd April I went down to London with Albert Best on the 10 a.m. train. Shortly after lunch, sitting facing each other on the train, Albert put down his book and in his excited typical stammer which I had come to recognise as the indication that he was getting something, he said, "Ann is just behind me, she asks me to tell you about the slipper". I said nothing and Albert paused for a few seconds as he often does while getting a message right. Then in more confident tone and slower and louder voice, "When your wife's personal effects were brought back from hospital were there blue slippers. No wait. There was only one blue slipper, the other was missing."

He continued in his confident tone as he seemed to see things more clearly, "Your wife is giving this as evidence, you understand? In your wife's toilet bag she says there were three complete sets of dentures which came back from hospital. She is also saying, Teresa. The same toilet bag had a blue container of talcum powder and a triangular small bottle of toilet water." Albert continued, "Your wife was with you this morning when you took out a large silk handkerchief and used it to wrap something in. This morning before you left the house". "Now," said Albert, "she is singing a song which you should recognise. She is singing 'C'est si bon'. She is going now but she says as she goes she knows about the Royal Stuart tartan."

Here indeed is concentrated evidence. Nothing vague but precise facts, one after another. First the blue slipper. This evidence was completely accurate. One blue slipper only came back in Ann's effects from hospital, the other was missing.

There were precisely three complete sets of dentures in Ann's toilet bag returned from hospital. (How many people would take four sets of dentures to hospital—the set she was wearing and three spare sets in her toilet bag? Yet Ann had always had trouble in getting dentures to fit well. She had four complete sets and she took three spare sets to hospital and the three sets were in her toilet bag returned from hospital. I should also say that I was completely unaware of how many sets of dentures she took to hospital or how many were in her plastic toilet bag, I really didn't feel inclined to go through her personal toilet bag when it came back from hospital. I had no idea of there being three sets of dentures there until I checked on returning home.

The name, Teresa, is Ann's mother's baptised Christian name. She has never used this name since she was married. She was always given the name, Daisy. Yet sometimes as a joke Ann used to call her mother, Teresa.

The blue container of talcum and triangular bottle of toilet water was in the bag as described.

At nine o'clock that same morning, in my home alone, I took out the only silk handkerchief I possess, a large white silk handkerchief and used it to wrap the microphone of my pocket tape recorder to protect it when I placed it in my travelling case. Albert had never seen this handkerchief at any time. "C'est si bon" was one of Ann's favourite songs which she used to hum. Finally, a week earlier Ann's mother and sister had bought a Royal Stuart tartan large travelling rug as a cover for the sofa.

Bearing in mind that Ann's purpose was to produce evidence, evidence, and more evidence, this is really concentrated material. I would be inclined to say that this sheer quantity of evidence becomes in itself a category of quality. One has to see Albert Best in his mediumship to be convinced that whether or not he is deluded, he believes that he is seeing someone who is giving this information. At

58

times he will say things like, "Repeat that," "Don't come so close". In the case of proper names he will sometimes say, "Tessie? No, that's not it, Bessie. No, I've got it, it's Nessie. I heard the 'Essie' part but I couldn't make out the first letter.

After observing Albert Best over a considerable time, I am convinced that the difficulty in hearing, clairvoyantly, some words and names is genuine and that he really sees, not with outward vision, but in some 'inner' way the people he describes.

I now come to my sitting with Ena Twigg, that most impressive and unassuming person who played a large part in convincing the late Bishop Pike in the truth of survival and communication. My sitting with Mrs. Twigg had been booked two months earlier. When I arrived at the semi-detached suburban house in Acton I met this very charming housewife who enthused over her flowers and spent almost an hour chatting about her life as a medium and introducing me to her husband. After an hour or so, Mrs. Twigg said, "Well, let's go upstairs and see what we can get". She sat relaxed and silent in the small upstairs study while I sat a few feet away adjusting my tape recorder. "Are we ready? Right!"

"Distinctly I hear a voice saying, 'I'm his mother'. She is one of the most outward going, charming souls I have met. No thought of self. She says that she has two sons. She has brought your father and a lady Jane or Jean. She says I want to tell you that you are just about to start on one of the biggest adventures of your life. Work towards September. You will be used as a person as I am being used, to break down the barriers. You will reach from your church to us to break down the barriers. Who is Wally?

"I'll have your photograph." (This I produced in a sealed envelope.) "This is someone you like very much—a lady— hands stretching out to you. She hasn't been over there very long. 'I was so tired.' It's your wife. She's only a few months over, less, was with you over the Christmas time. 'I just slipped out at the end and it was all over. I looked at my body because you came to see me. You stood at the bottom of the bed.

" 'I had to go to a hospital. They gave me injections and they gave me oxygen. Darling, I'm all right now. God bless you for telling me it was true. You've got my ring and my gold watch. And my clothes are still in the wardrobe. The coat with the fur collar.' She wants to thank you for the flowers you put in the house, for her.

"You didn't take the funeral service after all! They helped me to come along and I listened to all the nice things they said. Your mother helped me greatly. It was the most wonderful experience to realise that not only was I living, but I had no pain, no pain at all. Thomas à Kempis, *Imitation of Christ,* let me say it.

" 'I had trouble with my hair before I passed.'

"She says that she is in the house so much. Before she passed she used to like to look at television. 'I forgot that I was ill and tired because I could look at television and forget my pain and breathing.' She liked the children's programme so much.

"Don't lose your thread, go on, don't worry about names if you can't get them over. She says, 'You've already felt me near you when you were going to sleep. I kissed you good-night and I touched your forehead. You used to do this for me and you used to tuck me in before I went to sleep. Tuck my back in.

" 'It's been so much easier for me because you've been so brave and you've let me go free as a bird.' She's got a beautiful mind, this person. She loved her home. She was a person that did things in the home. She would make her curtains.

"She loved literature. She shows me piles of books. Books everywhere. She shows me also some poetry. Glasgow Infirmary she says, they were going to operate but they couldn't. Two young people, a boy and girl that she is interested in.

"The name of Ross is being called very clearly. Do you know if her mother is 77? She has one of her parents in spirit. Tell her mother that she's seen her father. Her mother is troubled with her feet. She passed over near someone's birthday, her own birthday. She shows me a card.

"She is a lively person. She says you're incorrigibly senti-mental. You looked through the snapshots the other day. You've been married twenty-five years. She thanks God that we had that opportunity to celebrate it. But what do we want to worry about twenty-five years for when we have all eternity to work it all out.

"The happiest day in her life, she says, was when you two met and it was love at first sight. 'We never looked at another person once we first met. That means that we belong. And it got better and better as time went on. We got to understand one another, and it wasn't the spoken word but togetherness and sharing, sharing, sharing. I can't cook your porridge now, but I can care for you in every special way that God gives me.'

"'You looked at my scarf. My dressing gown is hanging up. The one with all the colours. I liked pretty things. My weakness was I loved beautiful things. But I loved beautiful people too, beautiful inside.' She loved music, she liked to play the piano. 'Just know that the Bright Ones have helped me to find my way back to you.'

"I never was lost, you know. I was in despair before I passed over. I realised that I wasn't going to get better and I said to you, "I don't think I'm going to get better" and you said, "Oh, yes you will". But we didn't deceive one another, did we, and you held my hand, you sat by the bed and held my hand. After I had passed you kissed me, you kissed me twice.'

"She speaks of her sewing machine. She used to get impatient with it. 'Now I've learnt to be patient. To Kelvingrove, I like Kelvingrove.'

"'You were so strong when I was ill. You know how I loved the flowers, I always had many flowers, and I liked to do them myself, and it was the wee flowers I liked.' And another thing, the place is well kept."

I asked the question, "What was it like when you awakened?" " 'I had taken another good new breath. I awoke and saw my father and your father and mother and I said I must tell David I haven't left him.'

"We talked about this so often. I had a little photograph of Bill. I'm not a bit lost. I found a sure path. Very busy learning more about music.' She loved colour. Everything is a kaleidoscope of the most exquisite shades.

"She had a pink bed-jacket. I see her. She always tried to make herself look a little better when you came in. It was very bad here, is this the right spot? (Points to centre of chest, retro-sternal.)

"We went to Edinburgh. We liked Edinburgh.' She didn't like killing. 'I'll be with you in September.' She couldn't bear a lie, this woman. She says 'because I looked for truth and expected truth I am among truth.' You have her spectacles in the case, two pairs. 'Not that we ever had to wear sun spectacles so often. We were meaning to go on holiday last year but we couldn't go.' She admired character more than anything. This girl will only come through a person she wants to come through and you're going to find she's going to be very selective. She is so sensitive herself that she couldn't bear to be represented as anything other than what she was and is.

"She's got lovely eyes and a naughty little chuckle. Not a loud laugh, not a giggle, it's a chuckle. Do you still like eggs? There is some joke here about eggs.

"Why do I want to talk about Lawrence of Arabia? (A naughty little chuckle again—to make you think, she says.)

"A birthday soon. Yes, today is a birthday. I gave a present to someone today. A lady? Yes. Wish her well will you?

"She is talking about Mary. Give Mary her love, tell her not to grieve. 'I'm wonderfully happy. With just the difference, you won't be able to see me, but you'll feel me'."

Here the sitting ended. I have tried to write almost a verbatim report from my tape of the sitting, excluding only some personal expressions of affection which would not be evidential.

I would say that the expression of Ann's character is almost perfect. An almost embarrassing truthfulness and an even more embarrassing expectation of truth from others. A love of beautiful things. This is not simply a stock phrase, she had the most exquisite taste in period furniture and old porcelain. She loved paintings and could spend the whole day in a gallery, hence here reference to Kelvingrove—the Art Gallery in Glasgow which she used to visit and when she became too weak and breathless to climb the stairway to the gallery this was her greatest regret. To be cut off from her beloved French Impressionists. I can remember her weeping at the sheer beauty of the words and the sublime outreach of thought in Plato's *Symposium*—"A deathless beauty". She used the phrase once to describe the speech of Socrates in the *Symposium*. Her own painting in oils has a delicacy—a sensitivity. I think it would be true in a sense in which it would be true for very few people, to say that she loved beautiful things. And beautiful people. Beautiful inside.

Character meant more to her than anything else and for herself it meant enduring, often being alone, often in pain and never complaining.

Ann was the most sensitive person I have ever known. Sensitive to a nuance of speech; to a change of tone. Sensitive to the quality of a touch or a handshake. Sensitive to a quality of the light or a subtlety of shade. Above all sensitive to people. She was totally incapable of rebuffing anyone, so sensitive was she to the effect of hurting another person. To someone who did not know Ann the above impression of her character might seem like a generalisation. to me it is the most perfect summing up.

Ann's description of her passing, in hospital, having oxygen. My coming to the foot of the bed. My kissing her twice*. All this is accurate. The joke about eggs refers to my habit of eating two rolls with a fried egg in each every week when I visit her mother. The reference to her terminal illness. She did say that she didn't think she was going to get better and I did say, "Oh yes, you will!" and really neither of us was deceiving each other. We both knew that it was the end and I held her hand that last night for hours.

This sitting with Mrs. Twigg had all the quality of a re-uniting and almost every word of Ann's was in character, every memory correct. I can only say that if this is a dramatising of material in my subconscious mind, tapped by the medium, then perhaps my whole marriage and all its memories was a dramatisation of material in my subconscious. Mrs. Ena Twigg has a gift of mediumship which, when it is attuned, provides a narrative quality to the material given which is consistent with the personality communicating. This is a very rare gift in mediumship.

I am sometimes asked, how does one become a medium and are most mediums just trying to make money. Here in Glasgow, my native city, anyone may book a half-hour sitting with any of Scotland's top class mediums. The charge for half an hour is fifteen shillings of which seven and sixpence goes to the local church where the medium is demonstrating

*Not at the hospital, but when she was in the funeral parlour.

63

and seven and sixpence to the medium. As most mediums need a short rest between sittings and probably arrive at 10 a.m. to begin a forenoon's work, a top class Scottish medium will have earned 30/- by 12.30 p.m. or roughly 10/- an hour, which in 1970 is less than a tradesman is paid.

Since sittings are only booked on two days following the Sunday service, I cannot see many mediums making more than £8 to £10 per week, including their fees for platform demonstrations on a Sunday. Compare this with the £10 which a minister earns for his Sunday's pulpit supply for one or two services and you will have an idea how ill rewarded mediumship is in the provinces.

It is only a sense of dedication and a desire to bring a measure of comfort to others which motivates the few dozen sensitives in Scotland at any rate, to go on travelling and demonstrating and giving private sittings, week after week, year after year.

In many cases a medium's gifts have only developed slowly over twenty years or so. In the case of Albert Best, his gift took over twenty years to develop to its present quality. Moses said, "Would that all the Lord's people were prophets." In this present age they would surely be ill rewarded.

Mediumship is not a money-making business and there is no competent professional medium in Britain today who has spent less than ten years in the development of mental mediumship and most have been much longer in preparation to reach their present standard of competence. This is one good reason why quality mediumship is rare, even if one happens to be born with a special psychic gift, few persons are prepared to undertake the discipline of development. There are probably many people in home circles who would never contemplate public mediumship. Until the established churches are prepared to recognise mediumship as they recognise healing, as a gift of the Holy Spirit, mediums will be few and poorly recompensed.

I look forward to the day when I shall be able to say to a bereaved person who will not be comforted by the standard reassurances of the church, "All right! I'll arrange for you to have a sitting with Mrs. So-and-so. It will cost you a fee of three guineas and if you cannot afford this the church will pay." This day is surely a long time ahead when this could be the official attitude of the church. Endless committees of enquiry would deliberate for years and probably shelve their report in the end. But there is no reason why individual clergymen who are convinced of survival and communication should wait for that day. It is no heresy for a minister to bring this assurance of survival and communication to a bereaved person.

7

At this point it should be made clear that although I am dealing with the evidence given me by Albert Best in a considerable part of this book, I am not on close personal terms with him. During the last six weeks I have only spoken to Albert Best by telephone and then only when he telephoned me. In many of these telephone calls Albert Best asked me for information or advice, particularly in relation to orthodox churches. In a measure, I think he valued my advice in relation to his own mediumship and when invited to take a meeting before a new type of audience he would sometimes telephone me and ask me what I thought about it. Thus I found that I was often giving Albert Best the kind of pastoral, indeed third party outsider advice which a minister often gives to church members.

Although Albert Best telephoned me, I very rarely telephoned him, unless it was for the purpose of trying to arrange a private sitting for someone. From the very beginning I made a point of guarding against the danger of being on familiar chatting terms with Mr. Best because I was always conscious of the over-riding necessity of reducing to a minimum the possibility of conveying information to him. After over twenty-fie years experience of psychical research, I am at least aware of the danger of saying in someone's company such remarks as "Ann and I loved that tune" or "We had a wonderful holiday there, once". It may sound calculating, but I have throughout this period and before it, always been aware that the unique mediumship of Albert Best would be the keystone of much of the evidence of survival which I hoped to make available to others. Thus the necessity of keeping myself aloof from this gifted medium, not to cloud the value of the evidence.

I have never, so far as I am aware, reminisced about Ann or referred to anything in my past in the presence of Albert Best. This is not to impute any dishonesty to him, it was simply the natural precautions which a person familiar with the value of evidence in psychical research would take. It is also worth emphasising that no member of my family or my wife's family has ever met Mr. Best, with the exception of one occasion when I took my brother (a doctor and a minister of religion) and his wife, to a group sitting a year before Ann died.

I know that there will always be the objection, on the part of the critic, that the very fact that each week, each month, there must have been a certain increase in familiarity with Mr. Best weakens the evidence. My answer is, of course, it does. One of the greatest psychical researchers of this century, Rev. Charles Drayton Thomas, sat regularly with Mrs. Osborne Leonard for almost thirty years. This is one of the factors which weakens all good evidence. The intelligent psychical researcher is aware of this difficulty. Yet at the same time, he realises that going from total stranger to total stranger among mediums, while it would strengthen the value of the evidence, it would weaken the quality of the evidence. The quality of mediumship depends to a great extent on medium and sitter being relaxed. To a certain extent they must believe in the integrity of each other.

Let the reader put himself in the position of a medium giving a private sitting for the first time to an enquirer. Most mediums are women. While there is always someone in the vicinity, usually the adjoining room, in a properly conducted private sitting in a Spiritualist Church, nevertheless confronted in a private interview or sitting with a total stranger, a man whom she has never met before and who might be a sexually obsessed person, or a newspaper reporter doing a series of articles on Spiritualism for a sensational journal, what is this woman's reaction? Can she possibly be relaxed enough at a first sitting to produce good evidence? The remarkable thing about mediumship under these conditions is that any worthwhile evidence at all is produced at such sittings. Yet, not only has some of the best evidence come to me at first sittings, but it has been produced in spite of adverse conditions.

It is no reflection on Spiritualism to point out that mediums are sometimes aware that they have a person sitting with them who really needs mental treatment. It is equally true that in any orthodox church a minister is sometimes aware that persons who come to him with certain types of problems, really need mental treatment. Indeed, my former Professor of Practical Theology instituted a series of attendances at psychiatric clinics in a local hospital for divinity students. There they could 'sit in' as it were and see a consultant psychiatrist at work. Not, as my professor used to say, so that we could become amateur psychiatrists, but that we should be able to recognise the pattern of the typical person who really needed mental treatment.

The same type of person is also likely to arrive at some time at a personal interview or sitting with a medium. It is no reflection on either the orthodox church or on Spiritualism to be aware that such people do exist. But it is one of the factors which make it unlikely that the best evidence will be obtained at a first sitting.

Equally, from the other side, the point is often made that the communicators too are acting under abnormal conditions. Familiarity with a particular medium and her guide or control helps considerably in producing the best type of evidence. Thus the wisdom of Mrs. Ena Twigg and the quality of her mediumship. She spent an hour chatting with me—never about my personal affairs—simply showing me her flowers, introducing me to her dog while she fed him with chocolate. I am convinced that if she had noticed signs of impatience or had any doubts about my mental state, she would not have invited me to begin the private sitting. All this is understandable and very wise.

From this it should be clear that in most of the best evidence, a certain familiarity with a medium will be inevitable. I am aware of the objections. All I can say is that I guarded against this objection of familiarity as much as possible, indeed I probably leaned heavily the other way in keeping Albert Best at a distance purely for this reason.

At the beginning of May I took one of my church members, the same person I had previously taken, in my car to the sanctuary where Mr. Best and others offer spirit healing. One of the women in the group, whom I only know by name, put on a tape of background music. When the tape was playing I was aware that most of the music was light music from musical shows, not the usual hymns which I had heard before. After half a dozen or so excerpts the piece of music which came on was "Lara's theme" from the film, "Dr. Zhivago". Now this piece of music has more significance than any other music of the last five years to me. Among modern themes it was Ann's favourite. I couldn't say how many times I have heard her playing it on the piano or how often she would hum this piece of music; she loved it!

Albert Best meanwhile was treating a patient who was lying on the plinth. The music came to an end. Suddenly there was a loud noise from the corner of the room near to the window. A bang, as I would describe it. Albert Best looked up. "That noise—your wife is here and she says, 'Do you remember the times I played that music and do you remember when we went to see Dr. Zhivago together. I influenced the woman to put on the wrong tape, the one with our music and I managed to make that noise, just to let you know that I'm here. I waited till the end not to spoil it for you'."

The following week I took the same person in my car to the spirit healing sanctuary once again. During the interval I had been in London. Once again, in trance and while healing, Albert Best said, "Who is Mrs. Murray, East Kilbride," addressing me. I replied, "That is my wife's sister". "Ah, yes!" replied Albert Best. "Your wife was talking about her. She says that she was with you when you posted a postcard to her sister when you were in London. You posted two postcards at the same time, on Monday of this week. She also says that she was with her sister when she got your postcard."

After a short pause, "You had fish before you came out here, sole, and it wasn't Dover sole. Your wife says you cooked it in a pot and you didn't clean the pot properly. Clean it again when you go home, will you?"

My comment on the Dr. Zhivago theme, known as "Lara's theme", at no time have I ever indicated Ann's love for this music to Albert Best. The fact that we went to the cinema together and saw Dr. Zhivago, indeed it was one of the last films we enjoyed together, was known to no-one except myself.

The postcards—I did post two postcards together from London. One to my wife's mother and one to her married sister at East Kilbride. I posted them on Monday of that present week. Every detail is accurate here. The remark about the fish. Just an hour previously, before picking up my member whom I took for treatment, I made a rough meal at home. I cooked two smoked soles in a pot of water. As I was in rather a hurry, it was a rushed meal, tea, bread and butter and the sole. I then cleaned the pot quickly and rushed out to keep my appointment.

When I came home again I took out the pot and looked at it. I had put it back in the cupboard. The pot was smelling strongly of fish and there were marks on the side, traces of fish still there. It would certainly be true to say that it was not properly cleaned.

I cannot escape the growing certainty that Ann is still here. That under these exceptional circumstances she is able to make her presence felt. The remark about the pot not being clean was probably made because it was in character and she was always very fussy about keeping food vessels scrupulously clean. The details were not only true, but the incident was completely in character with Ann as I remember her after twenty-five years together.

8

About this time I gave an interview to *Psychic News* in which I spoke of my convictions of survival and communication and gave examples of one or two of the most impressive pieces of evidence since Ann's death. Incidents in which I felt that she had returned and produced the kind of evidence which at least could not be explained on the basis of telepathy. In the interview to which *Psychic News* devoted most of its front page, I said that "My ministry is enhanced by the fact that when I enter a home where, as often happens, the shadow of bereavement has come, I do so with the certainty that death is only the opening of a doorway. I know that the so-called dead are more alive than we are. They are not further away from us but closer to us." I went on to say that I found most church people were "eager, hungry for any experience which makes the Bible more clearly understandable. Above all, I find that confronted with the challenge of death, people are secretly longing for clear and decisive certainty." Most of the interview was taken up with examples of the evidence contained in the four months since Ann died.

What I had said as a Church of Scotland minister I felt I had to say. I honestly detested the embarrassment and the publicity. As someone in my congregation who heard of it said, "A minister should behave with dignity. To flaunt the story of his wife's spirit return in a sensational Spiritualist weekly is brash and insensitive. I trust that if bereavement comes to me, I shall keep my grief private and any comfort I receive also private." This remark is typical of the kind of criticism which I have received. I felt that I ought to reply to such criticism in my Whitsunday sermon.

I said, "This is Pentecost Sunday, the birthday of the Christian Church. Supposing there had been a *Jerusalem Daily Recorder* published at that time, what would it have said in its headlines the following morning? 'Rowdy Scenes

71

in Upper Room' would be the caption. 'Followers of the recently executed criminal, Jesus of Nazareth, were involved in an hysterical outburst yesterday. Some witnesses of the strange incidents claimed that most of the persons concerned were drunk. "The whole episode was disgraceful," said one eminent Pharisee—Saul of Tarsus—who was asked to comment, "These people should be imprisoned."

" It was claimed that some of these followers ofthe Nazarene were in a kind of trance or control and actually spoke in languages which they did not understand. People in the crowd claimed that they recognised sentences in Egyptian, Sanskrit and Persian. One follower of the cult described to our reporter strange phenomena in the upper room. Tongues of flame, fire, and a rushing wind. Asked to comment, His Grace the Very Rev. Caiphus—High Priest of the Temple—advised people to keep well away from this hysterical cult, "It could be dangerous".'

"Well, that's how our church, the Christian Church, started. If you had been one of the readers of the *Jerusalem Daily Recorder,* which side would you have been on? Do I need your reply?

"Fire was the sign of the beginning of your church and fire stands for danger. The first sign that God is using you is that you stop worrying about what people think about you and you worry about what Christ thinks about you. That means danger.

"Paul speaks about his life as a Christian and he says, 'In danger of trials, in danger of fastings, in danger of shipwrecks, in danger of false witnesses.' In danger, danger, danger. What is the opposite of danger—safety? What is the safest job in the world today? Being a clergyman like me. My salary is guaranteed. I cannot be sacked or dismissed by you, my congregation. I am admitted *ad vitum aut culpam,* that means, for life providing I don't run off with someone in the choir.

"I can bore you stiff every Sunday. I can reduce my congregation to a few dozen members sleeping in the pews. I can totter up to this pulpit until I am ninety-five if my legs carry me, and still I will be paid either by you or church headquarters if we have no money.

"Do you think it right that the representative of these rowdy, excited people in Jerusalem, in danger of their lives, should be in the safest job in the world? Too much safety is like too much money. It eats into your soul. You can never get enough of it. You begin to hoard money not when you have too little but when you have too much. Then you die with thousands of pounds stuffed into stockings and into drawers and leave a fortune to some ill-deserving second or third cousin to drink and dissipate. Too much safety has the same effect. You begin to hoard safety. You can never be safe enough. You worry about every action, every word, every public statement you make, in case it offends someone and they might leave the congregation. What nonsense. As though the Almighty cares a jot whether you worship Him in St. Andrews-on-the-green or St. Thomas-on-the-hill.

"So clergymen become almost afraid to speak because of too much safety. What started with the good news that 'Death is swallowed up in victory,' shouted in rowdy, hysterical joy, becomes a dull charade. Every time I am in doubt about doing something which may offend someone but which in honesty I believe to be true, I remind myself that "safety is the cancer of the church".

I quote at length from that sermon because it was and still is my honest reply to the safety brigade in the church.

At the same time as this, following my interview in *Psychic News,* I began to get letters from church members, most of them Church of England, about a dozen Church of Scotland. One person, after a tragedy so unbelievable, wiping out his whole family said, "I even feel that my minister is embarrassed to come. When he calls he is embarrassed and I am embarrassed. He has nothing to say and he feels it, I am sorry for him. Nothing in my church has any meaningful answer to the question that is breaking my heart, where are my family now? Is death really the end and is all my twenty years of church-going just an accumulation of words. Believe me, I have prayed, and prayed, and there is silence in Heaven. Can you help me?" This and a pathetic letter from a man, a church elder for forty years who ends his letter, six months after the loss of his wife, with the words, "Do you think there is a chance?"

Such letters have come to me and heaven knows how many other clergymen and mediums get such letters. At the same time what of all the tens of thousands of hearts that do literally break in silence and write no letters. Surely the

Orthodox churches have to be condemned for their failure to comfort those who mourn and to make real the great doctrine of the Communion of Saints and the ministry of angels.

The letters take long and careful replies and in each case I have offered to give the writer two or three hours of my time so that we can have a long talk about the problem of survival and communication. After the person has satisfied himself that the evidence is sufficient to point strongly to the fact that his own dear ones are in fact living in another dimension and that they are unchanged in every respect, except that he no longer sees them with his physical sight, then ought to begin the deepening of his spiritual consciousness.

The emphasis from the other side is that struggling for position, acquiring things, valuing others by outward appearance, is in fact the basic illusion of living. The constant urging that we should find a place in our lives for silence and meditation, simply to be still and be aware of ourselves and of this other dimension and of the peace which comes in stillness, this cannot be other than a strengthening of orthodox religion and its basic doctrines.

Then again, from the other side comes an equal emphasis on service. This again is no encouragement to be other worldly but on the contrary a strong insistence from our loved ones and from guides that each one of us has a purpose in living and that it is part of a higher plan or God's will that we should fulfill our purpose, that we should live our lives here, to the full, and that we are only half alive when we concentrate on making money and acquiring possessions. Jesus said so in the parable of the Rich Fool. He was a fool because his life had no motive beyond acquiring more and more possessions. The knowledge of the dimension of what we call a supernormal world which is in and through this physical world and a part of it and, yet infinitely more than it, and from which our loved ones unchanged and with their love for us unbroken are still in contact with us, can only enrich the traditional doctrines of the churches. The tragedy is that orthodox churches have for so long been afraid of God's gift of knowledge. They have worshipped God with all their hearts, but that is not enough, they must worship too with all their minds and this can mean giving up many stubbornly held positions.

It is encouraging to realise that the Church of Scotland was the first church in the world to take seriously the question of psychical research and its bearing on religion and in 1922, long before any other Protestant church considered the question, its Committee to Investigate Supernormal Physic Phenomena consisting of eight Professors, one Law Lord (Lord Sands) seventeen ministers and two medical specialists, reported on a majority report to the General Assembly. *"Investigation is lawful. The Church has welcomed the sure advance of knowledge in the physical sciences and is hopeful that the Soul of man will soon be better understood."* That in 1922 was a brave statement and one of which the Church of Scotland, my own church, should be very proud.*

At least the Church of Scotland was more honest than the Anglican Church which also set up its committee to study the question of Spiritualism in 1937. The Anglican committee was appointed by the Archbishops of York and Canterbury to report on The Church and Spiritualism. After a decent interval no report was forthcoming. Enquiries were made and it was learned that the House of Bishops had taken the odd decision not to publish the report.

For nine years this report languished, then suddenly the majority report signed by seven of the ten members of the commission appeared in the office of the editor of *Psychic News*. The editor at that period got in touch with a member of the committee whom he knew was in favour of the report being published, though bound by his oath of loyalty to keep its secrets.

The member of the committee agreed to read the report and at least correct any mistakes, in the interest of truth, since it would be published in any case. The report was returned with every comma clearly marked and missing lines written in the margins. The report was then published in *Psychic News* and extracts, with the co-operation of the Press Association appeared in newspapers throughout the world.

From the Church of England there was silence on the

*For the complete text see Appendix 1.

substance of the report and only a protest from the Archbishop of Canterbury that its contents had been divulged. He did not deny the accuracy of the report. Why a great church should stoop to the back-handed method of suppressing its own report is open to anyone's interpretation. The attitude of mind in the 20th century which believes that its bishops have a right to decide what is good and what is bad for ordinary members is authoritarian. The signatories to the report which recognised the probability of the Spiritualist hypothesis and that in some cases messages did *recognition of the nearness of our friends who have died* come from 'discarnate spirits' made some interesting comment. The report expressed the opinion that *"The and of their progress in the spiritual life and of their continuing concern for us, cannot do otherwise for those who have experienced it than add a new immediacy and richness to their belief in the Communion of Saints.*

Regarding guides, the report says *"The belief in angelic guardians or guides has been very general in Christianity."* The signatories to this majority report were Dr. Francis, Bishop of Bath and Wells, Dr. W. R. Mathews, Dean of St. Pauls, Canon Harold Anson, Master of the Temple, Canon L. W. Grenstead, Nolloth Professor of the Christian Religion at Oxford, Dr. Wm. Brown, Harley Street Psychologist, Mr. P. E. Sandilands, Q.C., Barrister at Law and Lady Gwendoline Stephenson. On the whole a rather balanced and powerful cross-section of the Anglican church.

The Church of Scotland is a much more democratic institution by its Presbyterian form of government which recognises the parity of all ministers and an equal number of elders to ministers in its higher courts. It publishes its reports of commissions in advance of the meeting of its General Assembly each year. It received the majority report from which I have quoted and although this report may lie buried in the files of its College Library acquiring dust and cobwebs fifty years later; nevertheless, it is the voice of the General Assembly on this question of survival.

I therefore always emphasise to the church member who comes to me that whatever disapproval he may encounter from individual ministers, there is no question of heresy; neither in the Anglican church nor in the Church of Scotland. Most members are not aware of this and feel that to enquire into psychical phenomena is somehow being heretical. Proper warnings should be given as to the danger of enquiry without expert advice and guidance and the emphasis that proof of survival is only the beginning of the individual's realisation that his true destiny lies in a closer knowledge of God in Christ and that survival is only the beginning of the Life Everlasting. There is no reason why orthodox churches should fear psychical study and the confirmation which it gives to some of the church's sorely tattered doctrines today.

9

On Monday, the 11th May, I had a sitting booked with Mrs. Findlater, with whom I had sat on two previous occasions. As usual I took my cassette pocket tape-recorder, a necessity for any serious investigator of mental mediumship. It enables the sitter to switch on and sit back and relax. The constant strain of trying to write notes in long hand and to keep pace with a fast talking medium is enough to reduce a sitter to the verge of collapse and to produce irritability and to adversely influence a sitting'.

It is also not fair to mediumship to judge a sitting by what you can remember later. I have proved this. The names and important references left out of notes of a sitting compiled afterwards from memory can amount to almost 50%. Unless an enquirer can review the contents of his sitting with a medium at leisure and even play it over to some relative or friend who often points out an obvious reference missed, he cannot claim to be seriously investigating this subject. I therefore switch on my recorder, check that it is operating and sit back relaxed. Here are the salient points of this sitting.

First I am introduced to a Dr. Cassels who had a connection with an aunt of mine. I know of no such person but I had an Aunt Mary who was a midwife in Kirkintilloch forty to fifty years ago and she knew a number of doctors there. I shall have to check on this.

My wife comes now, Ann. The name is given clearly as Ann, your wife. Ann refers to a group around me and gives the name, Lawrence. (This is the name I have been given so frequently.) To my surprise, she says, "But you must spell it 'Laurence' with a 'u' not a 'w'. You will be shown the other way."

Now follows a quite accurate description of my brother's home and situation. Ann is the communicator. "Your brother is making a change soon and he is worried. He is hoping and praying it will work out all right. She is saying 'Yes! He has made two changes already in the last five years, but this is the best change which lies ahead.'

"Your wife is speaking about three young people in your brother's home at present. (This accurate. At present my brother's two daughters aged seventeen and twenty-two are at home and also the older girl's husband, also twenty-two, whom she married five months ago. The married couple are living at my brother's place meanwhile until their new home is ready to move into.

"It's the younger child your wife wishes to talk of. She says that the younger lady has been in some doubt about an examination recently. There are two papers and she has doubts about the first one. Tell her that she has just made it. This young girl is very fond of animals. She reminds you that she was this girl's godmother and she has a special interest in her.

"Now Ann speaks of the older girl. They are two different natures entirely. One is fond of horse-riding. The older young lady is a sensitive person and she has a creative gift, but she is not putting it to good use at present.

"Now for your brother's wife. Ann says that she has a condition of nervous debility which needs attention here. There are two conditions working together which she is afraid she will not overcome. Tell her that first of all she has to take the pills but that she will be all right. Ann is also speaking of George in this family link."

My comment on this evidence so far is that every point I have mentioned is specifically correct. My brother was at the time in the course of joining a new medical partnership. He had just resigned from the partnership where he had been for the previous twelve months.

He was very worried about making this decision and as he admitted later to me, hoped and prayed that he was making the right decision. That was my brother's third change in the last five years. He had changed from medicine to the church and back from the church to medicine again (two changes), now he was about to make another change. This was exactly the words of this medium who claimed that Ann was speaking.

The references to my brother's two daughters. The younger one had sat her University Entrance Higher English a week earlier and felt she had not done too well. The previous day she sat Higher French and felt more confident. This was described with precision by Ann. This younger girl, Eleanor, is passionately fond of animals and would like to be a veterinary surgeon (accurate). Ann was her godmother (accurate).

The older girl was a competent horsewoman and liked competing in jumping events. She is very artistic but has really neglected this talent recently. I would describe her as very sensitive. (All most accurate again.)

My brother's wife has been suffering from nervous strain in recent months and although she has been given tranquillizers such as Valium, she is reluctant to take them. (Accurate again.)

The reference to George. This is the third young person, the husband of my brother's elder daughter, living with them at his home meantime.

Now comes the question—Did I give a subject on the *Book of Job* recently? I replied, "Well, I suppose I do preach on the *Book of Job* from time to time." Ann, through the medium, insists, "No! That is not what I mean. You used it only very recently. Just think." Suddenly it struck me that when I was having dinner with Maurice Barbanell, editor of *Psychic News,* in London a fortnight previously I had quoted to him two texts from the *Book of Job* as examples of the beauty and wisdom of this Old Testament book. They were, "These are but the fringes of His ways, how small a whisper do we hear of him" and also "Friends should be kind to a despairing man, lest he lose his faith in the Almighty." "That's it", said Mrs. Findlater excitedly, Ann is nodding her head and laughing. 'Just to let you know that I was there too and enjoyed the conversation.'

"Have you trouble with your hearing? Your wife is talking about your hearing. She says, consult your brother about it. (My hearing has been deteriorating a little recently and I have lately been aware of head noises.) Here Ann breaks off and refers to someone called Service whom my brother knows and asks me to tell him to get in touch as he may be able to help.

"Now! Does 'Softly awakes my heart' mean anything special to you?" (I should think it does. It was one of our special favourites and I spent days at one time searching for a recording of Marion Anderson singing this aria from Samson and Delilah. Ann and I both loved this record and played it regularly.)

Now my mother takes over. "She says that you have been deleting and repeating the same words again." This is true. I had been writing an article and after deleting a paragraph decided to put it in again exactly as it was.

Now Ann returns to give me the name Carmichael which she says has a link with Canada. "You don't know anything about this name," she says, "but I give it as evidence of something you are not aware of but which you can check with my mother, who will remember it". (Two days later I visited Ann's mother and asked her if she remembered anyone, now dead, named Carmichael who had a link with Canada. "Of course," she replied, "long before you met Ann we knew the Carmichaels. They emigrated to Canada and I heard since that Mr. Carmichael died there.")

"Now Ann refers to the fact that her mother is not too well." This is the first time in all her communicating that Ann has spoken of her mother's health in this way. (Exactly a week earlier her mother had taken a heart attack, not too drastic, but sufficient to be alarming.)

"Ann says that she is concerned about her mother and much of the trouble is that there is a lack of interest. She has lost the will to live and yet life holds quite a lot for her if she could just be shaken out of this depression." (This again is an exact description of part of my mother-in-law's problem.)

Suddenly I am given, out of context, the name of Ross with the remark that Ann is smiling and seems to treat it as a joke. "We will inspire you ourselves, you know."

"You wound up my watch the other day, for the first time in months, but once is not enough, you must wind it every day if you want to keep it in good condition." (Perfectly true. I wound up Ann's watch the previous day, for the first time in three months.)

"When you bought that new recorder," (I had bought a new cassette pocket recorder a few weeks previously), "you relaxed and spoke into it. Your guide was there and when you played it back you heard a word spoken twice which startled you because you didn't remember saying that word. The word was OM—OM or God." (This again is startling.

81

I did speak a little poetry and some nonsense into my recorder and thought it curious that I had spoken the word OM twice. I concluded that I must have said this word out of my subconscious without being aware of saying it. Yet the voice did seem strange. Yet here almost a month later a woman, Mrs. Findlater, claims that my wife is speaking to me and that a group of those on the other side were responsible for this word which startled me on playing back what I had spoken into my recorder. No living soul knew of this except myself.

At this point Ann spoke of Lawrence—I assumed that it was some reference to Lawrence of Arabia. We had both shared a keen interest in his life. Then she said. "But you must spell Lawrence with a 'u' not a 'w'—Laurence. I could make nothing of this item.

"Have you got a little piece of stone moulded to a Dutch shoe?" No. But I discovered that Ann's friends Mr. and Mrs. G. did have a porcelain Dutch shoe and that Ann had once admired it.

Now Mrs. Findlater declares they are showing me a sign of an Eastern temple—a Buddhist temple where you would take off your shoes before entering. "They say that this temple is a symbol which you will be given. It will all fit together. Remember it is one of our symbols."

Now there follows a description by Mrs. Findlater of a person who claims to be a guide. "He is a Franciscan monk. Tall, gaunt, and he gives his name as Brother Nicholas. He says that France meant much to him, so long ago, so long ago. He says 'I will help him'." Nicholas may have been his own name. I don't know.

Finally Ann says that she is progressing and not nearly so conscious of her breathing. This was a hangover from the years of breathlessness, so that even after her passing she still felt a little frightened to do things. Now she is getting over this. "I've cast off so much that was a burden to me. Yes, I still require help but I am able to communicate." My mother breaks in to say, "You see, Ann really lived very often in spirit conditions, when she was in bed and alone, so much so that she has adjusted very quickly."

"Your mother was a very God-fearing woman," says Mrs. Findlater. "She is saying with a smile, 'Yes—but your father was and he wasn't. Sometimes I had trouble getting him to go to church. Nevertheless, he had his own thoughts of God. When she wanted him to go to church he would rather potter around at home. They are both laughing."

This is an exact description of my mother and father as I remember them. Mother loved going to church but it was always an event when she persuaded my father to accompany us. Here the sitting ended.

Let us consider at this stage where the evidence has led us so far. There is a mass of second class evidence. That is, there is a considerable amount of specific items of evidence transmitted by one or two mediums, notably Albert Best, that either my wife, Ann, or some part of a medium's personality has access to two classes of information.

First of all the memories which Ann and I shared. This consists of such remarks as, "She is reminding you of the time when you saw the film Dr. Zhivago together," or "Does the music 'Softly awakes my heart' mean anything to you?" This we may call 'shared memories'. It can never of itself be proof of survival. It is always open to the objection of the sceptic that these memories remain buried in my subconscious and that in a certain condition of what we call mediumship, they can be tapped by a sensitive, who may be temporarily in an abnormal condition of consciousness which is commonly called trance or being over-shadowed by either a guide or secondary personality.

The important thing to remember about the type of evidence which we say may be explained by telepathy is that, while this is a fair criticism, the telepathy hypothesis is still a fundamentally weak one in this context. When it is used to explain the type of evidence in which a complex piece of information is given (i.e. "Do you remember the time when we returned from a Gilbert and Sullivan opera and I lost my diamond ring in the car and we found it again three days later? The opera was *Iolanthe*.") Thus even the telepathy explanation goes beyond any form of telepathy so far demonstrated under scientific conditions. All too often we find that the critic who invokes telepathy as an explanation for so-called communications from post-mortem personalities, on other occasions is very reluctant to admit that telepathy exists at all.

Secondly, there is the other type of second class evidence which is distinctive from 'shared memories'. This is the claim on the part of someone from the other side. I hate using the term 'disembodied spirit' because 'disembodied anything' is a concept which our minds cannot entertain and even St. Paul refused to entertain such an idea. This is the claim that 'they' from the other side are aware of what we are doing at a particular time and can tell us of things which we are doing or have done, of which no living person except ourselves is aware.

Closely identified with this is also the type of communication which points out some little detail, perhaps something out of place at home, or missing, of which we are not aware. This gives us the strong feeling that an invisible presence is able to be in a room with us and even note details in the room of which we are unaware. If we admit that some extension of a medium's personality is able to do this, we may weaken the case that it is our own loved one who is communicating, but at the same time we considerably strengthen the 'prima facie' case that human personality survives bodily death in some form. If some part of our personality is able to travel over distances and be in a room and notice details such as 'stains on the hem of a curtain' which escaped our notice, then it is unlikely that this part of our personality is wholly dependent on our physical bodies.

There still remains the first class evidence. This is the kind of statement which is made by Ann, as communicator, on a number of occasions, where she tells me of an incident or fact in the past which was not known to me and not known to the medium. The incident of the ballet shoes is a good example of this. Here we have strong evidence that Ann is, as I believe, trying to produce evidence which excludes the categories of telepathy which we can imagine might operate and produces her private memories which I did not at any time share and which I can still verify from another living person. Very often this other living person has to 'dig deep' to remember the incident. It is not always on the surface of their memory.

All this has taken place in roughly four months from the time of Ann's passing. It is accompanied by a dramatic quality when describing Ann and her personality. There is the characteristic way in which she used her fingers and hands in emphasising a point. The sheer number of items alone is impressive, since hardly a day has passed without some further piece of evidence. I feel that if this were not the most highly charged emotional issue in human existence, the case for Ann's survival would be accepted by others as it is accepted by me. But proof and evidence are two different things. Proof is the condition when no possible alternative hypothesis can be put forward. It is doubtful if such a condition can be conceived while the human mind remains fertile and imaginative. Evidence on the other hand is the accumulated build-up of facts pointing in a certain direction. The time comes for each one of us when we 'burn our boats' on the basis of evidence, never of proof.

To each partner in a marriage I would say: You married on the basis of evidence that you loved each other, not of proof. Proof belongs to the exact sciences where emotion is not a factor. But we live by making that leap, which is an emotional one, from evidence to belief. So it is in the quest for survival and communication.

On the 22nd May I took my friend, Mr. D., for his usual weekly healing session at the healing sanctuary where Albert Best attends and offers healing. I have noticed that it takes sometimes as long as ten minutes before Mr. Best is completely in trance and controlled by the entity called Hans. Sometimes in the event of the case being particularly difficult, this entity Hans steps aside and allows another control known as Dr. Wong to take over. During the course of healing, which may involve manipulation of limbs or simply the laying on of hands, it is common for this control Hans or Wong to turn around and address an unseen communicator. In this instance Albert Best, while controlled by Hans, turned to me while I sat with a dozen other persons, waiting while my friend was receiving healing.

"Your wife is here again. She says that you have just lost a filling from your back lower tooth on the right side, a large filling and it is giving you trouble." Two days previously I lost the entire filling from my right back lower tooth.

"Now she is talking about a pillow. Not an ordinary pillow, a very special one — Dun — Dun — Dunlow — Dunlopillow, she says. She says that you have not got her Dunlopillow." I replied, "This is quite true". "No!" said Albert Best, "because she says it is still in the hospital. Why don't you go and collect it, you would sleep more comfortably with it." My comment on this is that the day before

Ann died she complained that the standard pillows in the hospital were too hard, and hurting her back and she asked me to bring in her own special Dunlopillow from home. At 5 p.m. that same evening I returned with her own pillow and put it behind her. After she died the pillow was not returned to me. It was true to say that it was still in the hospital.

Next came, "Your wife says in evidence that you gave away a picture a few months ago". I said, "Do you mean a painting?" The reply was, "No, a picture of your wife". Albert paused for a few seconds, "You gave the picture, she is saying, to the Gemmells". This again was correct. Two months earlier I had a number of large coloured prints made from a negative and mounted and framed. I gave one of these portraits of my wife to our friends the Gemmells. At no time since I gave this portrait to the Gemmells had they spoken to Albert Best—indeed they only knew him through me.

Finally I was told that my wife mentions that I had been in a restaurant in Castle Street, in Glasgow, recently and I enjoyed my bottle of wine. Ten days earlier I had dined in a restaurant in High Street which is an extension of Castle Street and did have a bottle of wine.

During this time Mr. Best kept remonstrating with the communicator who claimed to be my wife by saying, "I really must get on with my job here. This will have to be the last message." Right at the end he turned round, "Your wife simply won't go away, she asks me to just add this last piece of evidence. She was with you last night when you tried to sew on a button, the middle button on the coat of your suit." Once again this was absolutely correct. The previous evening I had made a rather clumsy effort at sewing on a button which had come off, the middle one of the three on the coat of one of my suits.

10

The theory that entities, including our loved ones, surround us and exist in a world which is as real to them as our world is to us, is the stumbling block for most people. The vast literature of Spiritualism contains hundreds of books containing accounts of this unseen world. Books like Anthony Borgia's *Life in the World Unseen* or Jane Sherwood's *Post Mortem Journal* are examples. They describe, with a remarkable consistency, a world in which one is usually aware of cities, mountains, lakes, gardens, houses, in fact a replica in some ways of our own familiar world, with the notable absence of motor cars and transport. One is usually met at the moment of transition by one's close friends or relatives and perhaps taken for some time to a place of rest or recuperation. Then follows descriptions of adjusting to this new life. Interests such as music, painting, philosophy may be continued in halls of learning, Universities of the Spiritual World, etc. Transport is usually described as simply willing one's self to be at a particular point.

Generally the descriptions of the qualities and diversities of sound and colour are such that they are more intense than we experience. At the same time there is generally agreement in this literature that this sphere to which most decent people eventually go, after death, is not the only category of existence. There are higher spheres of which they are aware and lower spheres where entities and personalities of evil and degraded nature find themselves. Exalted beings from higher spheres visit this intermediate sphere or dimension. There is a constant awareness of love and service to a higher and less egotistical existence. The nature of what we are destined eventually to become in no way contradicts the Christian belief in The Life Everlasting, which is a phrase describing the progress of the soul towards closer unity with God, both in this life and in the life hereafter.

D. H. Lawrence once referred contemptuously to Spiritualism as an attempt to 'suburbanise the hereafter'. It is always easier to coin an epigram about something than to understand it. It seems to me that in spite of the fact that part of our nature shies at the seeming absurdity of a world, beyond this visible world, which has its houses and rest homes and libraries and concert halls, we must take this description by communicators seriously. Let us remember that Jesus said, "In my Father's house are many mansions". "Mansiones," literally means stages of resting places for Roman soldiers on the march. If there are stages, surely the first stage after death will be a more or less familiar one in which the transition will be made easy for us.

The real difficulty has always been for human beings to conceive of an existence outside of a three dimensional solid space and a one directional time series. This point was always insisted on by Kant whose *Critique of Pure Reason* and *Critique of Practical Reason* still remains the summit of man's intellectual achievement in attempting to understand the fundamentals of human existence. The whole of New Testament and Pauline teaching on what happens after death is contained within the categories of three dimensional space and one directional time series. Hence the necessity to situate Heaven and to situate Hell or Sheol or Hades. Heaven is situated in Christian terminology in the sky, somewhere high, beyond all visible sight, and Hell under the earth or in some place removed in space from Heaven.

All this was a pretty secure cosmology until the middle of the eighteenth century, when this tight secure concept of Heaven and Earth and Hell began to crack. Immanuel Kant demonstrated that space and time are intuitional forms, a subjective condition of our knowing anything and that 'the thing in itself' as he called it, could not be apprehended through the spectacles with which we are born, namely three dimensional space and a one directional time series. The ground was beginning to tremble.

First of all Euclidian space, the space of pure geometry began to tremble. During the 1820's the Hungarian, Bolyai, and the Russian, Lobachevski, discovered that the Euclidian axiom of parallels was capable of contradiction. Then came the realisation that a curved surface like the surface of a sphere could present a geometry where, for example, the sum of the angles within a spherical triangle would amount to more than the classical 180 degrees. Euclidian space was crumbling as the only intuitional form of space. Now of course there is an unlimited number of mathematical spaces which can be posited by varying curvatures. All of them possess equal mathematical validity.

The idea that three dimensional space is merely one particular type of space among other possible types and that time as a uni-directional, one dimensional series, can no longer be held, has been familiar since Einstein's theory of relativity. Far from there being only one simple Biblical and Euclidian space of three dimensions and subject and object, the modern physicist and mathematician can conceive of other spaces and of curvatures in space-time. In short, we can go no further today than to say that a space, and there are many spaces, is a category in which things stand in a relationship to each other.

Prof. H. H. Price in one of his essays asks the question, "Where is the space in which we dream?" The mountains and rivers and people of our dreams, are they situated in an area located in a square inch of brain cells? The idea is absurd of course. In dreaming we enter a space which was always there, a dimension in which things stand in a relationship to each other. The intensity of our dreaming experience is no less real than any event in our waking life, while we are experiencing the dream. Yet the adventures and happenings take place in a space which we cannot intuit in our normal waking condition.

The possibility of the existence of other spaces than the space we consciously inhabit is not an absurdity in terms of modern physics. The old picture of the informed scientist laughing at the uninformed suggestions and imagery of another world which religion has so often used, is no longer applicable. In his book, *The Savage and Beautiful Country* (Chatto & Windus, 1966), Alan McGlashan quotes the words of Denys Wilkinson, Professor of Nuclear Physics at Oxford University in a broadcast, "Perhaps there do indeed exist universes interpenetrating with ours; perhaps of a higher complexity; perhaps containing their own forms of awareness; constructed out of other particles and other interactions than those we know now, but awaiting discovery through some common but elusive interaction that we have yet to spot. It is not the physicist's job to make this sort of speculation; but today, when we are so much less sure of the natural world than we were two decades ago, he can at least license it."

Alan McGlashan goes on to suggest that "the Dreamer, this mysterious guest who lodges in the psyche of every man, and for all we know of every living thing, may be one of the common but elusive factors which links us to other and higher-dimensional forms of existence?"

One might also ask, "Of what are the clothes we wear and the luggage and transport of our dreams composed? Are the ships and trains real?" We reply, "Of course not!" But that reply is always made on waking, when we put on the spectacles of Kant's three dimensional subject and object relationship again. Anyone who studies the writings of W. J. Dunne, such as his *Experiment with Time* or P. D. Ouspensky's *New Model of the Universe* or J. B. Priestley's writings on the problems of time, will have to admit that in dreaming we are faced with part of the problem of another kind of space or dimension. Priestley goes so far as to conceive of our entry at death into a new time-series where we have an existence and a range of possibilities. While Priestley would repudiate the Spiritualist position, yet I feel that it is in philosophy and terminology that he mostly differs. The fact that we may exist after the change we call bodily death is not called in question.

The purpose of this chapter is to assert that there is nothing logically inconsistent or absurd in the description of life on the other side of death. It seems to bear a relationship to the world we sometimes enter in certain types of dreams, with the difference that we have volition and are able to exercise will and purpose and motive to a degree not normally encountered in dreams. That this space or dimension exists in juxtaposition to our three dimensional space and one directional time series and may in a sense inter-penetrate it, means that our loved ones may, under certain conditions, be aware of our space-time dimension and see us in our homes and notice the little everyday things we do. It is no surprise therefore that they communicate and in evidence tell us of little things which to us are re-assuring and convincing of their presence.

Thus a great deal of evidence from Ann is of this type.

It is to me both logical and consistent and I can think of no other way in which I could prove my continued existence and love for someone if I were passed the barrier of death, than the way Ann has chosen.

The bulk of the evidence in this narrative has come from Albert Best and I have found his mediumship at its best to be more compelling evidence of survival than any other medium I have known. It is the sheer spontaneity of the information which comes to him which is so arresting. I have known an instance where Mr. Best (who is a football fan and enjoys going to Ibrox Park on a Saturday to watch Glasgow Rangers play) while talking animatedly about football with me, suddenly breaks off and introduces a phrase which comes to him. At the same time he is aware usually of the communicator who is giving the evidence. Typical of this as an example, in the midst of a light-hearted conversation Mr. Best may break off to say, "There is a William Watson here talking about a brass horse-shoe in his home, he seems to know you, will you try to find out?" Then the conversation continues. The above names and examples are imaginary but the instance is typical.

In describing this phenomenon, Mr. Best usually says that he doesn't hear the words as he would a speaking voice, rather he is conscious of the words 'in his head' as though they 'came into his head'. He is also conscious of visual phenomena. For instance when he is demonstrating platform mediumship he is aware of a 'kind of rod of light reaching out to the person for whom, in a vast audience of five or six hundred people, his message is intended. This in itself is a unique kind of evidence of survival for it strongly supposes that some purposeful intelligence is directing the medium demonstrating to a particular person in an audience of five hundred people. Not all platform mediumship is of this quality. Sometimes a demonstrating medium will simply announce a name and ask if anyone can 'take' this name and when someone volunteers will give further details.

When Albert Best is demonstrating at his most impressive, and understandably his mediumship varies according to his state of health and the condition of the audience, he can be most impressive. I have known him to come to a town where he was a total stranger. I recall once being present when he visited Ipswich from Glasgow and demonstrated before a large audience. On a number of occasions he pointed to a member of the audience whom he had never seen before and proceeded to give a detailed, accurate message. For example, in a totally strange town 400 miles from his home in Glasgow he pointed to a woman in the audience and said, "Your husband John is here and he wishes to remind you of the time one day in August, twenty-three years ago, when your Pekinese dog got lost and you both spent the whole night together walking the streets and looking for it."

The questions which arise from this remarkable mediumship are these: How was Mr. Best able to point first of all to a woman sitting at the back of the hall among 500 odd persons and without hesitation give this remarkable evidence? I may say that every word was confirmed by me as correct and the person concerned told me later that she was a total stranger to Mr. Best and had come to this type of meeting for the first time. There are, in explaining this incident, two distinctive items. One is, how does he single out a stranger among 500 other persons? How is he drawn to her? The other is: from where does he get the detailed evidential memories? Both together point strongly to the purposeful action of an invisible intelligence directing him as he describes it 'like a kind of ray of light' to the person the communicator wishes to reach. The accompanying detailed accuracy of the message given, together with the location of the recipient makes for a very impressive type of evidence.

There is another class of evidence which may occasionally be given in platform mediumship and this is the demonstration by the person claiming to communicate from the other side, of knowledge which strongly suggests an invisible intelligence linking two people together. For instance, about a year before Ann's death I addressed a meeting of about 200 people, under the auspices of a local Spiritualist church. Afterwards Albert Best demonstrated platform mediumship. First he described and named a person, Mr. B., an elder in my church who had died about a month previously. This person thanked me for my attention during his illness and for my conduct of his funeral service. I had concluded my funeral address with the words from *The Pilgrim's Progress,* "And all the trumpets sounded for him on the other side". The communicator, Mr. B. described by Albert Best as smiling and obviously joking said, "And tell my minister there were no trumpets on the other side".

Immediately after this remark Albert Best looked towards the back of his audience and said, "And by the way, Mr. B. your elder, says that he recognises someone else whom he knows in the audience. Quite decisively, Albert Best pointed to a woman wearing a red hat. "Madam, would you please stand up. Have you ever met Mr. Kennedy on the platform here?" The answer came "No!" Then Albert Best turned to me, "And have you ever met this lady?" I replied, "To the best of my knowledge, no!" "Well!" said Albert Best. "Mr. B., your elder, who is giving me this message, says that you ought to know her because she is a member of your church."

"Madam, are you a member of this gentleman's church?" The reply, "Yes! I am and Mr. B. was my elder many years ago, but I have moved out of the district some years ago and have not been able to attend except at odd times and I have never met Mr. Kennedy and he does not know me." Finally Mr. Best asks, "Have you ever met me before?" "No!" came the answer.

Now here we have a situation where an invisible entity claiming to be one of my church elders whom I had buried a month earlier recognises one of his old members in my church, and introduces me to her, although I did not know her name or that she existed. All this takes place in the meeting place of a local Spiritualist Church where I would least expect to find one of my members.

At his most inspired, Albert Best is probably the finest platform medium in Britain today. Here is an example of this type of outstanding mediumship. In a town 400 miles from Glasgow Mr. Best, as a stranger, points to a gentleman in the audience, "Do you know Mr. G.?" The reply, "I can't recall such a name". "Well, he knows you and he says that he lived at 122 S - - - - Street and was a sergeant of the police in Great Yarmouth and he sang with you in Gilbert and Sullivan over twenty-five years ago." What could be more specific than that?

A member of my church persuaded in survival and communication by Albert Best's mediumship so that her sense of the Communion of the Saints is greatly enhanced has told me of how, under tension and after being in hospital with a nervous complaint she went for a walk alone one summer afternoon. She was feeling at her lowest ebb. Walking through a meadow in the sunshine she suddenly cried out, addressing her father and mother dead these many years, "Where are you now that I need you?" A very natural and human cry in the circumstances.

About a week later this woman attended a demonstration of platform mediumship by Albert Best. Without hesitation he pointed to her and said, "Your father is here and he says that he was with you when you cried out, "Where are you now that I need you" a week ago. I find that this woman's belief in God and in our lives as being held in His loving purpose is enhanced by such an experience. It is my regret that so often I have the frustrating experience of knowing that I could help to minister the grace of God to someone by this sweet and blessed reassurance of the Communion of Saints and the Ministry of Angels and I am confronted with a blank wall, a wall erected by years of prejudice. The kind of prejudice which leads clergymen to speak in pejorative terms of The Witch of Endor, a 16th century solecism supplied only as a chapter heading by our witch burning translators. Yet even they cannot escape translating the Hebrew accurately in the narrative as, the woman of Endor.

It is also interesting that there is nothing in this Old Testament story which in any way reflects on the character of the woman of Endor. Indeed she is generous and solicitous towards Saul and emerges from the narrative as a perfectly kind and reasonable person who happens to possess psychic gifts.

The best and final commentary on such a story is to remind oneself that the account of the incident must have come from one of Saul's servants after the death of Saul and the oral tradition is passed on to some editor whose purpose is to discredit Saul and all his actions at that period. Since it was accepted that if Kings were defeated the Spirit of the Lord had departed from them; King David's adultery, murder, lies and theft are glossed over because he was a success, while Saul is represented as 'a lost soul' at the later period of his life because he was a failure.

The very fact that the Witchcraft Act operating against

mediums was only repealed in 1951* reveals the extent to which ecclesiastic prejudice has befogged the attitude of church members to psychic gifts.

As I write this chapter on 4th June 1970 I have been interrupted by a telephone call. It was Albert Best telephoning to give me a message from Ann. Curiously, I had been feeling rather lonely and depressed as I took up the threads of this narrative today. Here are the words I received over the telephone. "Ann is telling me to telephone you. Are you going to Eaglesham?" I replied, "Yes! I am driving out there on Saturday". Albert says, "Ann appears to be laughing about it." I replied, "Well, I'm taking a car-load of twelve to fourteen-year-old girls from my church for a picnic at Eaglesham." Albert replied, "That's why Ann is laughing. She says, 'Tell him I'll be going with him just to see that he behaves himself and tell him to cheer up'."

I am convinced that Ann was aware that I was a little depressed and took the opportunity of getting through to Albert Best, just to make the typical kind of joke which she would always have made and to assure me of her presence.

As I take up my pen again I am reminded of her words through Ena Twigg, "Just remember that I'll always be close to you and able to help you and work with you in so many wonderful ways, the only difference is that you won't be able to see me, but you will feel me."

*On 22.6.1951 the Government passed the Fraudulent Mediums Act. This act repealed the Witchcraft Act of 1735 and withdrew certain provisions of section four of the Vagrancy Act of 1824. Under the Vagrancy Act of 1824 Spiritualist mediums were lumped together with burglars, purveyors of indecent literature and persons guilty of indecent exposure and beggars, and were liable to prosecution under section 4 of the Act.

Under the new Fraudulent Mediums Act of 1951 a medium must be proved to exercise powers of clairvoyance or telepathy with intent to deceive and he must act for reward. No proceedings may be brought against anyone in England or Wales except with the consent of the Director of Public Prosecutions.

11

There is a curious piece of evidence in this series of communications which so far as I know has never before been the subject of comment or analysis. This is, in the case of the mediumship of Albert Best, the lapse of two months before the first sporadic messages from Ann begin to come through. I would describe Albert Best as pathetically eager to be able to bring me the comfort of a solid reassuring item of evidence from Ann in the two months following her passing and yet he was perfectly honest with me. "I simply get nothing at all, not even a sense of her presence." This is remarkably impressive. It would have been easy for a dishonest medium to have produced a number of unverifiable items in the familiar pattern, such as "She sends you her love. She is happy and growing stronger". Albert Best refused to offer me anything of this nature. "I can only be honest," he said, "I get nothing, no sense of her presence at all."

Now if the telepathy hypothesis is a valid one, or if the more elaborate and speculative theory that somehow a gifted medium has access to the forgotten memories of anyone who ever had any contact with Ann, be correct, the question arises, why should this extended telepathy or access to a universal pool of knowledge not operate from the moment of Ann's death? Why should there be eight blank weeks following Ann's death, when there is complete silence on the part of this gifted medium? If there are memories in my subconscious waiting to be tapped by a sensitive person, these memories are just as much present a few days after Ann's death as eight weeks later. Indeed since the best of the evidence from this medium has come without my presence, and has been given to me by telephone, why indeed the delay of eight weeks?

On the telepathic hypothesis this delay is unaccountable. On the other hand in terms of the descriptions given by our loved ones and others from the other side, this delay is understandable and consistent. In Geraldine Cummins' *Swan on a Black Sea* in which the principal communicator in the scripts is Mrs. Willet, there is a delay of almost three months before one of the subsidiary communicators begins to 'get through' for the first time. During the three months she is described by the other communicators as "sleeping a great deal and resting". There are dozens of similar instances in accounts of communication where the recently passed on personality requires a two- three- or even six-months period of adjustment.

In the very earliest communications from Ann she is described as being present but not able to communicate herself or even to tolerate the conditions of being close to this 'earth plane' or 'different dimension' for very long. All this carries a considerable weight of conviction as we trace the slow development of conditions where Ann no longer required my mother to act as intermediary. This is certainly not accounted for by any non-survival theory where the capacity to have access to information should not require a two months delay.

The reader of psychical literature will soon find himself confronted with a wealth of theory of the existence of the other world. Most of this literature will soon assume a familiar pattern in its descriptions of the world into which we enter at death, as being of higher vibrations than are normally apprehended by human beings. our loved ones' spirit bodies, the world they inhabit, the ranges of colour visible to them, are all vibrating at a higher rate than the forms of energy in vibration which we perceive as solid matter and visible light. It is, they say, a world of finer and faster vibrations of energy.

The time has come to give vibrations a rest in psychic literature. Anyone wishing to measure the strength of the orthodox scientist's critique of the vague use of 'vibrations' should read Sir Peter Medawar's review* of Tielhard de Chardin's *Phenomenon of Man* and his strictures on the un-informed use of the term 'vibrations'. With vibrations we encounter also beams of energy at velocities far in excess of the speed of light accounting for certain psychical

*In *Mind*, Vol. LXX, No. 277, January 1961

phenomena. Such vague accounts of the scientific background of psychical phenomena really weaken a perfectly sound case, as far as orthodox scientific thinking is concerned.

Any form of energy, such light, or any fundamental particle is subject to the basic concept of Einstein which has never been refuted. That as a body approaches the speed of light, its mass becomes absolute, i.e. its mass becomes the total mass of the universe.

The problem is not to look for an invisible world in terms of higher vibrations or velocities in excess of light, which are in my opinion, even when they come from scientists on the other side, only parabolic in nature and capable of fitting our three dimensional subject object view of the world through Kant's famous spectacles. What psychical research has really failed to appreciate is the impact of Modern Existential Philosophy on modern ways of looking at man's place in the universe.

From the time of Greek philosophy, through Hegel, right up to Kant's Critiques of Pure and Practical Reason, the emphasis has always been placed on *Essence*. That is, how could men analyse the nature of reality, including himself, to its fundamental irreducible essence. What was the reality, the prime essence behind all phenomena? That was Plato's problem and it remained the problem of philosophers right through the intervening centuries. As it came to an end with Kant's demonstration that the 'thing in itself' was unknowable, philosophy turned to another avenue, Positivism, Logical Positivism, Linguistic Analysis. Here philosophers began to divide statements into 'a priori analytic' and 'a priori synthetic' statements. Ultimately, they said, we are bedeviling ourselves by the very language we use and the questions we ask, which in many cases are not questions at all but just emotional noises we make.

Here philosophy seemed to reach a dead-end, until a completely new emphasis and direction entered into men's thinking. Instead of placing the emphasis of our search for reality on the Greek concept of essence, let us begin to look closely at this state which we call existence. Let us look inward instead of outward. So man, who in the western world had been preoccupied with the objective or essence, began to look inward into a new world, the strange world of his own existence.

From writers like Kiergegaard and even Pascal there seemed to point forward an inwardness in man which had been ignored. Some of this inwardness or existential examination was pessimistic. It saw man's being as surrounded by nothingness, non-existence. It saw man's essential dignity in being aware of his impending non-existence, of the surounding nothingness and facing with dignity the fact that his existence had no meaning, except for the meaning which man in his essential lonely and tragic destiny imposed on it.

It was left to Martin Heidegger in his famous *Sein und Zeit* (Being and Time) to clearly formulate the strange nature of human existence which had never been clearly formulated before. The first thing we are aware of is that we each possess existence, 'Dasein'. I also am aware of my existence as being different from any other person's existence. There is a quality of 'Geworfenheit', 'thrown-ness'. Like the throw of the dice I am aware and I ask myself why I should be thrown into this particular place of my existence? Why am I me? Why am I born an Englishman or a German or a West Indian? Why was I placed in this town born in this family of these parents? Existence has this quality of 'thrown-ness'.

There is also another important quality of my existence that is, the 'mineness' (Jemeinigkeit) of my existence. There may be 600 beds in the infirmary where I am lying and they may be all alike. Each with its same coverlet and pillow. Each with the same human shape in it. But one of these beds contains me and the world on which I look out from the body I call me is never the same as that of any other body.

It is my death, my suffering, my prayers, my tears, and because they are mine, because some non-objectifiable ego behind my eyes and observing my thoughts looks out on the drama, it can never be the same as any one else's drama. To someone passing by, there are 600 patients in the beds in the hospital. To me there is a unique intensity, a sense of destiny, an aloneness in that one body in which I lie, which is mine.

It is in Heidegger's discussion of the problem of death that the whole of his philosophy seems to focus. Here is a modern philosopher who really looks at death and dying in a way in which no philosopher has ever gazed on the problem before. Death is the one fact which sets a boundary to existence. To Heidegger, all authentic existence is 'being-towards-death' and to be able to face the fact of death rather than run away from it is authentic existence. The person who truly exists recognises this quality of 'being' as a movement towards death. Yet in contrast to Sartre there is almost a kind of joyful note in Heidegger's attitude and contemplation of death. It is the boundary of being but it is what gives being its significance.

One cannot escape the feeling that as Heidegger describes this quality of being, authenticated by death, it has something of the transcendental about it. He is not concerned wtih the question of survival and would probably regard death as annihilation and yet it is his concentration on existence and analysis of being and unflinching gazing and examination of death which is important. Heidegger is the philosopher who I feel most of all prepares men and women in this materialist age to look inward. He might even be said to bridge the gap between Eastern and Western philosophy; between the best in the Upanishads and Bhagavad-Gita and non-pessimistic existential philosophy today, because the attitudes are similar.

Heidegger, in his unflinching meditation and analysis on the state of being with its accompanying 'Angst' (not anxiety), and its movement towards death, calls inauthentic existence what Eastern philosophy would call Maya-illusion.

Heidegger draws attention to this condition of 'Angst' which is not anxiety about a particular event taking place or not taking place, but the basic condition of being human and being aware of the boundary which death places around one's existence. The death of one's friends and loved ones makes one more aware of one's own 'movement towards death'. Authentic existence is to be redeemed from this 'dread' as Kiergegaard called it. There is a similarity between this and the state of being delivered from Maya-illusion in Eastern philosophy. Both are achieved by an unflinching and honest and basically optimistic examination of one's existence.

Heidegger seems to me to tremble on the verge of being aware of this other dimension, this inner space. Why should this observing ego, aware of its 'thrown-ness' and of its boundaries and of its 'mineness' in this state of being or existence, be utterly dependent on the body of which it is also aware? Is it an intuition of the other space to which death holds the key, which gives this peculiar note of reverence, even triumph, to Heidegger's description of being?

Heidegger's broad analysis of thinking into rational or calculated on the one hand and introverted or primordial on the other hand, is interesting. Calculative thinking is concerned with the things which are 'vorhanden', to hand; that is with the rational thinking we do concerned with things. We change our jobs. We decide where to go for a holiday. We buy a new car. We emigrate. We decide to see about that filling in a tooth. Introverted primordial thinking is concerned with the nature of our being. It is meditation, but where for the Eastern mystic or the Buddhist contemplative, meditation is a process of passive concentration, Heidegger is concerned to provide for Western man a relevant mode of self-understanding which is not world-renouncing. He recalls man to awareness of the strangeness of his existence, to examining the categories which have been taken for granted. Both Eastern meditation and Heidegger's existentialism are concerned with the same end, namely, opening to man the dimension of transcendence. Whether the Christian calls this dimension of transcendence by the ancient anthropomorphic term 'God' or the modern 'ground of our being' as Tillich or John Robertson would describe it or 'authentic existence—Being' in Heidegger's terms, it does not matter. The value of Heidegger's philosophy of being, or existence, is that it comes closer to the position of the scientist today. It is he who brings us closer to confronting this space or dimension which science renders credible today and which is the fringe of what we call the 'transcendental'.

There may be many strange dimensions or spaces. Jesus has assured us that there are 'many mansions'. In them the concept of God becomes clearer. What I am concerned to develop is the concept that the first and closest of these spaces is that into which we integrate at death. 'Enter' would be the wrong word for we have entered it now and it has entered into our three dimensional space, since a higher or additional space always embraces the lesser dimensional space which it includes. Once again how wise the genius of the writer of Job, "These are but the fringes of His ways, how small a whisper do we hear of Him."

12

The foregoing chapter was written on Tuesday, 9th June, finishing the last paragraph at 4 p.m. At 7.30 p.m. I once again took the same member of my congregation, Mr. D., out to the sanctuary in the country, a few miles from my home, where Albert Best and a group of people combine in a healing service. Albert Best was controlled by an entity who often controls him while in trance and healing, a Chinese, Wong. He turned to me while engaged in laying his hands on a patient, "Your wife is here again and she wishes me to tell you that she has to go into the Halls of Learning. She has work to do and prepare for, so she will not be around you or around the home as often as she has been recently. She will, of course, still come to you, but not so often.

"Then, with a smile, she says, 'What about the coffee you made this morning. You know that it was too black, too strong. Not good for you.' You know that she would not have taken that coffee." This is perfectly true. I used a particular brand of coffee which Ann detested and in any case made it rather strong. She would have detested strong black coffee of this type and always felt that it was bad for me. Indeed, my doctor called some weeks earlier and, noticing the coffee, warned me that since my blood pressure was a little high I ought to avoid strong coffee. So this was a very typical and very solicitous reprimand from Ann for taking strong coffee which was bad for my health.

Then Albert Best, controlled by Wong, continued, "Two days ago your wife was with you when you had an egg, the egg was broken up, no, cut up, and you ate it and it was a bit 'off' she says. But you didn't want to offend the person who gave it to you." Two days previously I had paid my usual call on Ann's mother and since I was dieting I declined to join them at lunch. Instead I allowed my mother-in-law to cook me a hard boiled egg which was sliced between two thin pieces of bread. This was all I ate. When I tasted the egg I realised that it was a little 'off' but I ate it rather than give offence after it had been cooked for me. This account was absolutely accurate and lest it be objected that most people eat an egg each day, I would emphasise that this was the first egg I had eaten in two weeks.

Now followed two remarks which really astonished me. "Your wife says that today you were writing about 'Breaking through barriers of space' and 'Einstein's theory of relativity'." The reader can judge how accurate this is by going back a few pages. More and more Ann builds up this mounting certainty that she is close to me and that she is aware of many of the little things I do, particularly when I am writing or thinking about some problem.

Now follows a strange jig-saw. The references to Lawrence of Arabia and the remark by Ann at my last sitting with Mrs. Findlater. 'Laurence—but you must spell it with a 'u' not a 'w''. At this same sitting I was given the symbol of an Eastern temple and told that it was a symbol which I would find meaningful later.

I played the tape recording of this sitting to Mr. and Mrs. G., two close friends of both Ann and myself, when I was having dinner with them a week or so after the sitting. The following morning Mrs. G. telephoned me and pointed out that she had noticed a small paragraph in *Psychic News* about a reprinting of a book published twenty-five years ago called *The Shining Brother* by Laurence Temple. Mrs. G. immediately saw this as significant. "If you fit together the name, Laurence, which you got from Ann and the symbol of Eastern temple, you get Laurence Temple," she said. "Surely this is pointing towards the fact that you must get hold of this book, *The Shining Brother* by Laurence Temple and read it."

A week later I was visiting a friend and in the lounge noticed a bookcase beside the window. I can never resist browsing through titles of books and on the first shelf, third along, there was an old copy of *The Shining Brother* of the printing twenty-five years ago. I asked to borrow the book and wondered what I might find in it.

The following day Albert Best telephoned me. "At 3 p.m. yesterday Ann is telling me something about a book in a bookcase near the window of a room, first shelf and third book along, it is called *The Shining Something*." I replied, "Yesterday I came across a copy of a book called *The Shining Brother* just as you describe it." As I was very busy at this time in church work, it was some weeks before I had time to sit down and read *The Shining Brother*. I did at last have a free evening on Thursday, 11th June, and sat down to read *The Shining Brother*.

I had just finished reading the preface when Albert Best telephoned, "Ann is asking me to tell you that you have just finished reading something about Rev. Charles Thomas ten minutes ago." I had, ten minutes previously finished reading the introduction to the book which was written by Rev. Charles Drayton Thomas. I agreed that this was so. About half an hour later Albert Best telephoned again, "Ann says that you are still reading *The Shining Brother*. On page fifty-five you will find the name of someone we both knew." I looked up page fifty-five and found the name of Helen Hughes mentioned. Both Ann and I had known Helen Hughes before she died. Then followed the words, "You are to read on from there" and at the foot of the same page I read the words, *"For at no time will I leave you in doubt but proof upon proof shall be laid before you."*

Is this then all one fantastic assembly of coincidence? Or is it a vast and complex plot by someone who has shown himself too honest to offer me a single platitudinous message from Ann in the first two months and has always been scrupulously honest in my experience with him? Or is it, as I believe it to be, the varied, sometimes simple, sometimes complex and always consistent attempt of Ann to come and as she promised, try to break through the barriers of that inner space which we call the other side?

The book from which the foregoing was taken *The Shining Brother* has been out of print for the last twenty years and to the best of my knowledge I obtained the only copy in Glasgow. Also, Albert Best had no way of knowing that I had obtained this copy. I am satisfied that his allusions to this book came at least from some extra-sensory perception.

The next striking item of evidence from Albert Best came on the 16th June at 10.45 a.m. while I was dressing in formal black in preparation for a funeral service which I was about to conduct in an hour's time. I discovered to my horror that I had no clean, stiff, starched clerical collars left in the drawer where I usually keep them. Normally I send a stock of forty or fifty to the laundry at intervals and Ann always reminded me when my stock of collars was getting low. I was in the midst of hunting through a pile of old soiled collars, looking for a clean stiff one, when the telephone rang and the familiar voice of Albert Best spoke at the other end. "Are you in the midst of looking for a clean white clerical collar, because Ann is impressing me to telephone you. First of all to let you know that she was with you while you were looking for the collar and secondly to tell you that if you look in the bottom drawer of the chest of drawers, in the right-hand corner under some shirts, you will find three clean collars." I put down the telephone and looked in the chest of drawers, bottom right-hand corner under some shirts and there were three collars. I returned to the telephone and said to Albert Best, "Well, she's bang on this time, the collars were there exactly where you said they were."

Albert Best continued, "And she says, 'Do please send away the pile of collars you have already collected in the special box where you keep them. There are exactly twenty-three in that box now'." I counted the soiled collars in the box, twenty-three in all. Finally, Albert Best continued, "Just before you go, Ann says, 'You are going to take a funeral of a Mrs. H. in half an hour'. She says that she will be with you and that she helped her over at her passing last week."

All the above was perfectly correct including the name of the woman who had died and in this case the funeral was private and no intimation had appeared in the newspapers. As Albert Best has no connection with my church and no way of knowing whose funeral I might be taking, the whole piece of evidence is very impressive.

As though the above were not enough, Albert telephoned about a minute later and apologised, "Ann just wants me to tell you that John (your brother) borrowed three of your collars a few weeks ago. Get them back." This again was absolutely accurate.

During this period of five months which I have detailed in describing and analysing communications from Ann, I have in the main omitted a number of sittings with other mediums where the material has been non-evidential. I had in all twelve sittings with different mediums and most of this material I recorded but decided not to include because there was little of a striking evidential nature. In every sitting Ann came through and also my mother and the remarks made were the natural human expressions of concern and love. As evidence to others they are neutral but surely it is reasonable to expect two people who love each other to say the trite ordinary things. I remember how often during the Forces Favourites programme when persons who were separated from each other by the span of thousands of miles when given a few seconds to get a personal message across, mostly found that the words they say when words are so precious are phrases like, 'Keep your pecker up' or 'We are thinking of you always'. Why should the brief messages from beyond the veil be expected to be different? The one solid evidential fact which emerged from all my sittings with different mediums to whom I was a total stranger, often booked under a false name, was that each medium at least described and named my wife by her Christian name.

The interesting new awareness which has emerged from the communications of these months is how much emphasis Ann has placed on her prayers and my prayers for her. She has constantly assured me of how my prayers for her have helped her and equally she assures me that she continues to pray for me.

Now as a minister of the Church of Scotland I am not supposed to believe in or exercise prayers for the dead. That is, if I take the Westminster Confession seriously, which, thank God, I don't. I promised at my induction to accept it as a 'subordinate standard'. It is now so subordinate that I find it obnoxious in places. Yet the curious thing is that Protestants of the Reformed Tradition have taken the strictures against prayers for the dead more to heart than any advice of Calvin or Luther, simply because of the Westminster Confession of Faith. Praying for our loved ones who have passed on is the most natural and sincere prayer which we are ever likely to offer in our lifetime and to stifle the natural response of love is inhuman.

Beside this it is a misconstruction of the attitude of the stalwart of reformed protestantism, Calvin himself. He writes, "I hear that in the celebration of The Supper there is repeated a prayer for the departed, and I well know that this cannot be construed into an approbation of the Papistical Purgatory. Nor am I ignorant that there can be brought forth an ancient rite of making mention of the departed, so that communion of all the faithful being united into one body might be set forth." While Calvin always had to contend with fanatics and extremists in his own camp, it is clear from the above that he saw no objection to prayers for the dead, providing that they were not the object of any financial barter.

In the Apology for the Confession of Augsburg, the Lutheran Divines write, "We know that the ancients speak of prayers for the dead which we do not forbid." Luther himself said, "For the dead, since the Scripture is silent on the subject, I think that there is no sin to pray."

The Bible is silent on the subject, or to be precise the New Testament is silent on the subject. It is equally silent on slavery, yet the value set on individual personality and the brotherhood of all men before a heavenly Father, makes slavery unthinkable. It took many centuries before institutional Christianity recognised this contradiction. The silence of the New Testament on praying for the departed is no argument against such prayers.

I pray for a number of my loved ones each day. I make no distinction whether they are here with me living around the corner or if they are passed beyond my normal vision in the dimension we call the other side. I pray for the dead at funerals. It is honest, it is not heretical and it is as natural as waving goodbye. It is high time that Protestants realised that in having created this un-natural inhibition about praying for the dead on the authority of a seventeenth century solecism, they are diminishing the doctrine of the Communion of Saints.

However, although the Bible is silent on prayers for the dead, the early church is not. The epitaph of Abercius, Bishop of Hieropolis whose tomb was discovered in 1882 begins, "Abercius by name, I am a disciple of the pure shepherd who feeds his herds of sheep on the mountains and plains and who has great eyes that look on all sides. These words, standing by, I Abercius bade to be thus inscribed, 'I was truly living my seventy-second year. Let every fellow Christian who reads this pray for me.' This inscription dates from about the end of the second century A.D. Dean Farrar points out that it is the earliest Christian inscription 'of any length' which we possess and that it gives us a glimpse into the thoughts of the early Christians.

It is time that the Protestant churches realised that to pray for our loved ones whom we call dead carries fifteen centuries of authentic Christian tradition behind it. To prefer the transitory reaction of Puritan England of the seventeenth century, which was really a reaction to the constant threat of a restoration of Roman Catholic rule, is to allow emotion to supercede reason and tradition. After all, who today would wish to speak of the Pope as 'that man of sin, that anti-Christ'. Yet these are the words and this is the mood which fashioned the Westminster Confession. It is out of this atmosphere that the objection in Protestantism to prayers for the dead grew.

With regard to the question of survival and communication, in the main I am ashamed of the attitude which many of the orthodox churches have taken towards Spiritualism. Perhaps from the beginning Spiritualism was an unfortunate word by which those groups who believed in survival and communication decided to appeal to the enquirer. It immediately caused orthodox critics to react by naming it Spiritism, a pejorative term. Most of the references to Spiritualism as Spiritism are made by orthodox church critics. I have before me a statement 'What Spiritualism is', published by the Spiritualists National Union as a postscript to Dr. Malcolm's booklet, *Psychic Influences in World Religion.*

"Spiritualism is a universal religion based on the fact that man survives physical death and is able to communicate with those still on earth. Its truths give comfort to the bereaved, who are thus assured of reunion with all who have passed to the higher life."

Evidence for survival is overwhelming and incontrovertible. It comes to us from many sources and is vouched for by eminent scientists, philosophers and divines as well as by countless ordinary men and women.

Spiritualism approves of all that is best in Christianity and other world religions, while rejecting what seems to be false and without foundation. Spiritualists have no set of creeds or dogmas but accept in general the following simplified statement of the Seven Principles: —

1. Throughout the Universe there is a Creative and Sustaining Power—usually termed 'God' or 'Infinite Spirit'.

2. Man is a Spirit here and now and irrespective of colour, race or creed, is a member of a vast Brotherhood.

3. Man continues to live after death of the Physical Body.

4. Spirits in the higher realms can communicate with man still in the body.

5. Ministering Spirits are always ready to help and guide mankind.

6. Man is personally responsible for all his good and evil thoughts and deeds.

7. There is a path of Eternal Progress open to all.

The above seems to me to be a splendid and dignified statement of a religious viewpoint. Religion in its broadest sense has been defined as "The attempt of the individual to relate himself to the Universe." Surely then we might have expected from orthodox churches and churchmen the basic courtesy of recognising a different but nonetheless sincere attempt to find meaning and significance in man's existence?

It is sad therefore to find that my own Church of Scotland published in 1955 from its own press, the St. Andrew Press, a book by Rev. Edward T. Vernon titled *Where Grave Thy Victory*—a manual of consolation. In a chapter on Communion with the Dead the writer states, "The fact must be stated, however, and stated emphatically, that there is not a shred of evidence to support the assertion that the happenings in a seance originate in any way from the departed dead."

This nonsense after the majority report of the same church, "The Committee on Supernormal Psychic Phenomena" consisting of eight Professors, one Law Lord, seventeen Ministers and two Medical Specialists had reported,

1. "The Church cannot dismiss these phenomena with indifference."

2. "Ministers may even encounter rare genuine phenomena in the ordinary course of their duties."

3. "There is room in the larger life of the church for Christian Spiritualists whose special experiences have been sufficient to convince them."

In the case of The Church of England's Committee of enquiry, ten years before this book was published by the St. Andrew's Press, the majority report had been published unofficially and stated, "We think that it is probable that the hypothesis that they (i.e. messages) proceed in some cases from discarnate spirits, is the true one."

To state that there is not a shred of evidence is either to misuse the English language by not understanding the difference between evidence and proof or to be totally uninformed of the work of psychical researchers over the last fifty years.

This same book goes on to tell its readers that "mediums employed to act as intermediaries are not usually of a very high standard intellectually and sometimes even morally". This is the kind of arrogance which is so palpably unchristian that it simply deserves to be exposed. What kind of survey did the writer do of the intellectual standards of mediums? Names like Mrs. Willet, Eileen Garret, Geraldine Cummins, Ena Twigg render such a statement false. But even if this calumny were true, what does intellectual standards have to do with the claims of mediumship?

The really base part of the criticism is the assertion, 'and sometimes even morally'. This is a crude kind of *argumentum ad hominem* based on the fact that he has heard of fraudulent mediums therefore it is fair game to use this emotional attempt to discredit mediumship. I have met a great many mediums in thirty years' experience of psychical research and I have met the odd person with mediumistic gifts whose moral standards were questionable. But equally I have met hundreds of ministers of religion and I have also known the odd one or two whose moral standards were questionable.

Surely this attempt to defame a class of persons is contemptible. This book goes on to say that 'alleged messages from the dead never have any moral or religious value to speak of; if they in fact originated from the other side surely they would occasionally make some reference to God or Jesus Christ.' Of course mediumistic communications are full of such references to God and Jesus Christ. I have found in my experience that our loved ones when they pass over are aware of the reality and presence of Christ, though still an invisible presence. We would say that the Holy

Spirit is very real to those who have been brought up in this atmosphere and to think in such terms. Those who have never given a thought to Christian teaching do not suddenly change in another dimension. They continue to be much the same as they were in the body.

But for sheer unfairness we have to read the section on Spiritism in the book by Horton Davies called *Christian Deviations* and published in 1954 by S.C.M. Press. Here the tone is set in the first paragraph by telling us that "Spiritism, the belief that spirits of the departed actually communicate with the living, is often erroneously styled Spiritualism—but Christians repudiate this claim to spirituality, on the part of a cult which uses material proofs."

Surely Christianity was founded on material proof that Our Lord rose from the dead? Indeed Our Lord told us that our spirituality would be judged by material proof, 'By your fruits'. Surely the Good Samaritan gave material proof of his spirituality?

This book refers again to the Witch of Endor. Surely ministers might be expected to read their Bibles and discover that she is referred to as 'the woman of Endor'!

He goes on, "Christians must repudiate any conception of the after-life as an automatic rest-cure and not primarily as the blessedness of everlasting fellowship with God and his saints." I have over 500 books on the subject of communication on my shelves and over thirty years practical experience and in no case, either written in any of these books or in my many sittings over those years, have I ever heard a communicator or read of one, give the impression that the after-life is an 'automatic rest-cure'. Indeed it is the Christian Church with its hymns, 'For all the saints who from their labours rest' which gives this impression. The constant emphasis of communication is that there is work to do. Progress to be made. To die is to be aware of a wider field of challenge and responsibility.

After all, to really live in this life is to be constantly on one's mettle. The artist with a new idea to express, the scientist with a new theory to test. That is to be wholly alive here. The only difference when we pass over is that the panorama widens. The possibilities which were thwarted in this life, by bodily illness and physical poverty no longer apply. God becomes a far more meaningful concept and love a more profound reality.

The real poverty of Horton Davies' criticism is best shown by his choosing to quote from a statement by Dr. James Black on the Christians' bewilderment at the claims of Spiritualism. "With the best will in the world, I cannot understand why spirits, presumably purified from the clogging influence of the body, should choose to manifest themselves only or mainly to people of this order, (i.e. mediums). If they manifested themselves to saintly souls or to those who live on a high spiritual and mental level, I could at once appreciate this . . . Frankly, I am puzzled and disturbed by it. God has always chosen the finest instruments to proclaim his message."

This is a strange difficulty. Some of the most heavenly music and surely music at its highest is God's gift to men, was composed by absolute blackguards. Cezanne, Van Gogh, Gaugin were no saints but God chose them to enlarge man's vision of colour and form. A medium is just what he claims to be—a medium. A vessel with a particular sensitivity and the fact that this gift has not been bestowed on the Archbishop of Canterbury or the Moderator of the Church of Scotland is only a further proof of Paul's wisdom, "That God has chosen the weak things of this world and the foolish things to confound the wise."

Nevertheless, the fact that this kind of uninformed condescending and arrogant criticism of Spiritualists and the claims for communication and survival have so often been made by orthodox church publications, has had its effect on Spiritualists who, with justification, feel that they have been under attack always by orthodox churches. Therefore they have often responded by attacking orthodox religion as a fundamentalist, dogma-ridden, static church. This is equally not so. Spiritualists are guilty of not realising the fact that there is a deep, honest searching in Tillich and Bonhoeffer and John Robinson and a tremendous compassion in the church which finds expression in Christian Action and Christian Aid and Shelter.

13

On the 19th June I took my church member, Mr. D., who is crippled by rheumatoid arthritis to the healing sanctuary a few miles from my home where Mr. Best has his healing sessions. Albert Best is in a degree of trance during healing and the controls who are in evidence at these sessions are Hans or a Chinese called Wong. Who are Hans and Wong? I have often asked myself this question. Is it a case of multiple personality? Do Hans and Wong have independent existences? it is impossible to demonstrate whether or no these entities are as they claim, separate personalities. I can only say that I believe them to be so. I cannot think of any test it would be possible to devise by which the independent existence of Hans or Wong could be demonstrated. One simply gets the very strong dramatic impression that they are there.

During the session Albert Best, in control, said that Ann was beside him and laughing, laughing about a headache. "Why should she laugh about a headache? Did you have a headache recently?" I replied, "Yes, I awoke this morning with a splitting headache and had to take a couple of aspirins." Albert Best replied, "Your wife says, 'It serves you right!'"

Now, the previous evening and during the early hours of the morning I visited my brother. We talked and watched television. During this time I had a meal with him and a bottle of wine. Later I had a fair amount of whisky, rather more than I should have taken, for the result was that for the first time in years I awoke with a hang-over. I said to myself as I took the aspirins, "You fool, it must be twenty years since you had a hang-over like this. What would Ann have said?"

There was, needless to say, no possible way in which Albert Best could have known of this. Yet the atmosphere of Ann laughing and saying, "It serves you right!" was so entirely consistent with what she would have said, and she would have laughed at my hang-over, as she did. Albert Best continued, "Ann is now showing me a small bottle about 8 inches long with a green liquid in it and cardboard around the top. She says that she was with you at the time." An hour and a half earlier I had visited Ann's mother and sister. While I was there in their home I answered the door and was handed a sample bottle of washing-up liquid. It was a green liquid in a bottle roughly 8 inches tall with printed matter on a cardboard label around the neck.

The next point made by Albert Best: "Ann is speaking about a lace cover in your bedroom. It has been washed." I replied that last week my woman had washed the lace cover by my bedside table. Quick as a flash Albert Best replied, "Ann is laughing and saying, 'What do you mean—my woman?'." Here is humour and gaiety in the last two items of evidence. I found myself joining in the laughter and yet the humour was absolutely typical of Ann. Finally Albert Best said, "Ann is talking about £42. Just a little extra piece of evidence that she was with you." Four hours earlier I had drawn exactly £42 from my banking account.

It is a curious thing about almost all of these communications that Ann never gives me any item of evidence which I have in my mind that she might possibly give. I can think of some pet names we used towards each other. I often think of a period of our lives which might be summarised in a word or two. These things are in my mind. Yet the evidence I get is never what I expect. It is as though Ann were saying, "We are both aware of the objection of telepathy as an explanation therefore I will always try to provide at least items which are not in your conscious mind." I had totally forgotten the incident of the green bottle of washing-up liquid. I had to be reminded of it. I had put the amount of money I drew from the bank out of my mind. I had to count the notes in my wallet to verify this. Even the headache and hang-over were forgotten as far as I was concerned, until I was reminded of it.

I can think of quite a few personalities who have no real sense of humour. Yet the humour which is part of the dramatic quality of a personality, such as, "What do you mean, my woman?" or "It serves you right!" in comment on my headache, is absolutely typical and consistent with

Ann. She was always quick to see any point which had a lighter side to it and to exploit it. I am reminded of the mediumship of Ena Twigg when she described Ann's reply to something I said as, 'a naughty little chuckle'. That phrase was dramatically perfect and exactly described Ann's response to so many little teasing episodes, as I knew her, 'a naughty little chuckle'. This may not seem terribly important to the person looking for verifiable facts but to me it carries a perfect picture of Ann.

Of one thing I am convinced. The medium actually sees and hears, or senses what he describes. I am utterly convinced of the honesty of the principle mediums who figure in this account. What has to be determined is whether this 'entity' which the medium sees and hears, with the memories of Ann and the dramatic characteristics of Ann and the appearance of Ann (for she has been described accurately in detail) is a pseudo-Ann created by the combination of my personality and that of the medium, or the real Ann whose personality in some form and dimension exists and can be contacted.

What it is important to remember is that this entity, Ann, has memories which are unknown to me. She remembers and mentions names and incidents of which I am unaware and which can only be checked by me by referring to her mother's memories or those of other members of her family. It is also interesting that Ann and I discussed together before she died the pointlessness of messages which repeated what one might expect to hear, on the grounds that this was what one might describe as first degree telepathy.

If I am thinking that Ann might refer to me by a nickname familiar to us and she does so, the thought is at least in my mind. If Ann produces something which is not in mind (or at least on the surface of my mind) and I have to remember it, this may at least be described as second degree telepathy and remains a further step removed in probability from the telepathy hypothesis. Ann has used very little in the category of first degree telepathy because we were both aware of the objections to it.

14

We may find philosophers who have devoted no particular enquiry into the problem of survival and communication who can help us in our approach to the problem. Just as Heidegger turns our attention to the inwardness of existence and the strangeness of much that we take for granted, so another modern philosopher, Ludwig Wittgenstein, has drawn our attention to the pitfalls in our approach to questions of Science and Religion. He is concerned to point out that people tend to play a language game. They use words and make assertions in different kinds of ways. They make religious assertions as though they were scientific statements. They use words to admonish or approve without being aware that they are doing so.

I leave the reader to judge the importance of Wittgenstein's analysis for himself by reading the *Lectures and Conversations,* edited by C. Barrett (Blackwell, Oxford 1966). How important this is can be shown as one reads the statements made by scientists at conferences and seminars at which the question of E.S.P. has been raised. One is aware that even the scientifically trained person can react by approving or disapproving.

Let the reader consider the following sentence, "I believe he is researching in Semitic languages but he dabbles in Spiritualism". Now "dabble" in the Oxford dictionary means "To engage in a hobby". Yet one does not describe a person as "dabbling" in golf or in gardening. This word has come to have a special meaning of disapproval. I once lectured on Jung's theory of Synchronicity and was described as "Dabbling in the occult". One could supply a string of words which are used in this way, for example the word "cult", which is often applied to a group of people engaged in study or activity of which one does not approve. I have yet to hear of a churchgoer being described as dabbling in

Christianity, but if he crosses the street to a Spiritualist or Swedenborgian church he immediately "dabbles".

Wittgenstein makes us aware that much of the language we use in religion and in my opinion also in our attitudes to communication are survival are really inherent attitudes of approval or disapproval and misunderstandings of the role we are playing in the language game. We do not understand the use of the word "dabble" by looking up a dictionary but by observing how people behave when they use the word.

Much of the confusion in arguments on the subject of survival and communication is that the subject is partly of the order of religious belief, because it gives meaning to and regulates our life. It is also partly a scientific inquiry. To treat the subject as though it were wholly one or the other leads to emotional attitudes of approval or disapproval and misunderstanding. The pitfall for the scientist is using words like "repeatability", "laboratory conditions", "create the impression of", "control experiment". This implies that all phenomena should conform to certain patterns and if they fail to there is a reaction of hostility. Language helps us to feel secure but it may also hide the truth from us.

One has only to observe the kind of reaction provoked by such questions as "Do you believe there is anything after death?" or "Do you think the dead communicate with us?" to realise that the question is not of the same order of questions as, "Do you think this rain will affect the harvest?" or "Do you think the electrification of this railway line will speed up the service?"

Both are types of questions, but one type belongs to what Heidegger would call 'calculative thinking' and the other to what he would call "primordial thinking". When the two modes of thinking interact, confusion follows.

For instance, Professor Broad went so far as to say in a broadcast in 1957 that some of Mrs. Willett's scripts for example "do suggest a greater degree of survival than the mere persistence of an active psi component. They make it very hard," he said, "to resist the conviction that the mind of a certain person has survived the death of his body and is continuing to think and plan." This statement is made after a lifetime of psychical research and the placing of the material under trained philosophical scrutiny.

Wittgenstein would probably agree that this is as far as scientific thinking or logical thinking can go on the question. It can formulate possibilities and assess their degree of probability. But the leap from degrees of probability to saying I believe that so-and-so survives bodily death and that he has spoken to me from beyond the grave, is by its nature the same kind of assertion which the religious person makes when he says, 'I believe my life is guided by God'. At that point we start to hold a picture in front of us which is constantly encouraging us. Wittgenstein's contribution to the survival argument is to clarify the position of the sceptic and the believer. We each play a role in the 'language game' as he calls it. Sometimes the role has been thrust upon us and we have little choice. The important thing is to be aware of the pitfalls of the uses of language.

Perhaps this language game is best demonstrated by quoting a paragraph from D. J. West's book, *Psychical Research Today*, (Duckworth 1954). "An interesting case of a medium making use, apparently subconsciously, of unusual feats of memory in order to create the impression of spirit intervention was reported by an S.P.R. investigator, Mrs. K. M. Goldney. The medium was Mrs. Helen Hughes who frequently gave public demonstrations of spirit communication. She would stand on the platform and point out various members of the audience and give them 'messages'. In addition to the customary expressions of good-will these messages usually included mention of one or two names, supposedly relatives of the member of the audience being addressed. On the occasion in question, Mrs. Goldney was in the audience and Mrs. Hughes pointed to a friend of Mrs. Goldney who was sitting in the next seat, "There is someone here who has come for you; Bessie—wait (apparently listening to a spirit communicator)—Bessie White. Do you know Bessie White? Mrs. Goldney's friend did not know the name and Mrs. Hughes said, "No wait, it is not for you but for the lady next to you—indicating Mrs. Goldney. After Mrs. Goldney had rather hesitantly acknowledged the name, she continued, Bessie White and Alec—Alec White. Do you know him too?" Mrs. Goldney had had a private sitting with Mrs. Hughes two years before. While apparently in deep trance she had given Mrs. Goldney many names and allusions which did not apply at all.

Towards the end of the sitting she had mentioned two names, Bessie White and Alec White which Mrs. Goldney acknowledged, not because she really knew them, but because she wanted to see if the names would be given to her again at a later date. Mrs. Goldney attended various public meetings given by Mrs. Hughes but she never received any 'message' until this occasion, two years later, by which time she had forgotten all about the incident. It was only by looking through her old records that she was able to verify the origin of the two names. The incident is interesting because these names do not seem to have been a favourite standby, such as some mediums have for use with all and sundry. Moreover, it seems unlikely that Mrs. Hughes kept a written note of the names, otherwise she would have used them long before. The most probable explanation is that the association between Mrs. Goldney and these two names stuck in the mediums' mind as a latent memory which for some reason emerged from her subconscious years afterwards."

First of all, notice that the writer D. J. West has already prejudged the case. He introduces the account as "an interesting case of a medium making use, apparently subconsciously, of unusual feats of memory in order to create the impression of spirit intervention was reported by an S.P.R. investigator."

Now this is, to any unbiased person, a possibility, but only a possibility among other possibilities—one of which is also that the communications came from a genuine spirit entity. The account which follows does not rule out the possibility of the communications being genuine.

If Mrs. Goldney had a private sitting with Mrs. Hughes two years earlier and received the names Bessie White and Alec White what does she mean by acknowledging them? Presumably 'acknowledged' means that she agreed with the entranced medium or her guide that she knew these persons named. In other words, Mrs. Goldney misled the medium. I quote, 'not because she really knew them but because she wanted to see if the same names would be given again to her at a later date'. Two years later Mrs. Goldney is given the name Bessie White at a public demonstration of platform clairvoyance which again she 'rather hesitantly acknowledged'. In other words, she misled again.

Now I knew Mrs. Helen Hughes fairly well and sat with

her in private sittings many times and witnessed dozens of her demonstrations of platform mediumship. The first thing she always said to me was, "If you can't place a name, tell me so, and we can sort it out". I have never known Mrs. Hughes even once in platform clairvoyance to fail to produce more and more information about a communicator if the recipient of the message replied honestly, "I cannot place this name". I have frequently had experience of receiving from Mrs. Hughes a name which meant nothing to me. I told her that the name meant nothing and immediately she would produce more background. In other words she would never give up. She hammered and hammered with more and more information until the name was placed. Mrs. Hughes was constantly getting letters from people who could not place a name at the time but were given information to check on and again and again she proved to be right.

Mrs. Goldney, it appears, misled Mrs. Helen Hughes twice. In addition we have to take Mrs. Goldney's memory for the placing of these names on trust. Who is to say that Mrs. Goldney had not met or had some relationship with a Bessie and Alec White and forgotten, it happens to people frequently.

D. J. West's summary or should I call it the conclusion which he reached in advance and at which he at length arrives is "The most probable explanation is that the association between Mrs. Goldney and these two names stuck in the medium's mind as latent memory which for some reason emerged from her subconscious years afterwards."

Even this loose explanation has flaws, for how did Mrs. Hughes recognise Mrs. Goldney? Were there 500 or 1,000 people at the demonstration, or 2,000 as frequently happened when Helen Hughes was demonstrating? Where was Mrs. Goldney sitting? At the back or near the front? It is not easy to recognise a person in an audience of 500, I know this from experience, and much more difficult in a larger audience. All these problems are overlooked in D. J. West's conclusions.

I quote this at length to point out the extent to which the role we assign ourselves, compulsive critic or believer, can influence our account of an incident in the field of psychical research.

15

A feature of almost every lengthy communication from Ann has been her concern for her mother and sister who live together in East Kilbride which is about ten miles from my manse. In the last few months since Ann's death I have visited them at least once a week. At my sitting with Ena Twigg, Ann quite definitely refers to her mother's trouble with her feet. Now it may be argued that most elderly people are troubled with their feet. But in the case of my mother-in-law, she had never been troubled with her feet in any way until two weeks prior to that sitting, when for the first time, her ankles began to swell.

At the sitting with Mrs. F. on the 11th May, Ann referred to the fact that her mother was ill. The actual words used on my recording are, "Your wife is really concerned about her mother's health. Something happened a few days ago. They are doing all they can to help her, but there are difficulties." I pointed out earlier that exactly a week previously my mother-in-law had a mild heart attack. She made fairly good progress and on Wednesday, 20th May, Mary, Ann's youngest sister, who is married and also lives in the area, telephoned me in the evening to tell me that she had visited her mother and sister that day and her mother seemed much improved. On the following morning at 10 a.m. Albert Best telephoned me and said, "Ann is impressing me to telephone you. She says that her mother was ill last night and had a restless night. Will you go up and see her?"

I drove the ten miles, rather doubting if this time Albert Best had not got a wrong impression. After all, I knew that everything had been well the previous day. When I arrived I found my mother-in-law had collapsed and was looking very ill again. The attack had started at 7 p.m. the previous evening and she had been sick and faint all night. Like many elderly people she had a dread of sending for the doctor, as she didn't want to go to hospital. I was able to get a doctor and help to calm her and the outcome was that she was ordered to stay in bed for a week or two and given medical treatment.

Since then I have recordings of three sittings with three separate mediums and in each case Ann refers to her mother's health. In one case, "She is a lot improved but she still has the pain in her face and neck and chest—tell her this will go away." In another sitting, "She has been ill but is improving. Tell her to stay indoors and not try to go out meantime. She needs more rest yet." Finally, "She is progressing but she will not be the same as she was before, she will have to be very careful, both in what she eats and in not overtaxing herself. I rely on you to keep an eye on her and to help her in every way."

This is to me very strongly indicative of Ann's concern over her mother as I knew her. She, of all the family, was most concerned about her mother's welfare and always made sure that in the summer at least once a week we should take her for an outing to coast or country. During the last few years Ann made a point of spending at least an afternoon and evening each week with her mother. Even when I had to carry Ann upstairs to her mother's home and it meant that Ann used all her energy in this weekly visit and virtually spent the remainder of the week in bed, Ann never gave up this weekly visit. She showed a greater than average concern for her mother.

This concern has come through in every sitting of any length and the impressing of Albert Best to telephone me when her mother took another attack, so that I could go there before I went out on any pastoral business (indeed, I had intended to be in Edinburgh all that day and was about to leave when the telephone rang) all this makes a very convincing and consistent piece of evidence for the continuing concern of those on the other side for their loved ones.

Towards the close of the last session which I reported at his healing sanctuary, Albert Best, in trance, asked me to step aside so that he could speak to me privately. Ann has brought forward someone who needs your help very much. His name is C— and he says that he lived at S—. Here he mentioned the name of a village on the coast of Scotland.

This man is a minister like yourself. His name is Thomas C—. He gave his full name and address. Now I didn't know anything about this minister. I had only known him casually in my previous presbytery and as far as I was concerned he was still alive. Albert continued, "Ann is helping him to come forward. He passed over some months ago. He wants you to tell C—, his wife, and W— and A— his sons, that he is all right, not to grieve and give them his love."

I checked up by telephoning someone in the area and discovered that G.C. had died some months ago. I have since discovered that his wife's name was correct and that the names of his sons were also correct. So far as I know there is no source from which this information could have been obtained. I was totally unaware (a) that this man was dead, (b) that he had a wife who was still alive, (c) that he had any family or of their names if he had any family. I cannot see how a medium could have obtained this information from any human source.

He might have kept files of all the ministerial deaths in the *Glasgow Herald* but from there on the rest of the evidence baffles human explanation. How did he know that I had even remote connection with the deceased person?

During these healing sessions at Capelrig where Albert Best treats patients there may be between ten and twenty persons present. I am not the only person receiving these messages. Commonly a person coming for the first time whom Albert Best has never met before will receive a message. Therefore the evidence coming from Ann is only part of what is sometimes a flood of messages in the course of an hour or two hour session. When Albert Best comes out of trance he is quite unaware of anything he has said. Indeed, on one occasion he made an appointment with a patient for a special session of treatment the following afternoon. Ten minutes later, out of trance, he said in conversation that he was going to watch a football match tomorrow. "But you are coming here to treat so-and-so!" "Oh! Did Hans say that?" I am convinced that this total blank during the time Albert Best is in trance, is genuine.

On Friday, 26th June, I took my church member who is unable to walk more than a few yards, for treatment. In trance Albert Best spoke to me. "Ann is here again, she is saying something about Sauchie." (This is a village in Clackmannanshire.) I replied that yesterday I had officiated at a wedding where the bride came from Sauchie. He continued, "The groom was another Kennedy, not you, Iain." I agreed that the name of the groom was Iain Kennedy. Next followed, "What did you do to the best man?" "Ann says that you did something discourteous but not intentional to the best man!" This was absolutely true. I absent-mindedly closed the official reception without giving the best man the customary opportunity of replying to the toast to the bridesmaid. I had to apologise and re-open the proceedings so that he could make the speech he had prepared. Fortunately it was all taken in good part.

"Ann says you must attend to your socks and buy a few more pairs. You had a hole in one that you wore at the wedding." Again true. To my horror I discovered at the function that a hole was showing above the heel of my shoe. "There is something wrong with your shoe which you are wearing. Take it off." I took off my shoe and discovered that the sole was separating from the upper part on one shoe. This was totally invisible and could only be seen by probing at the joint of upper and sole with a pencil. Still more remarkable facts were to come. Albert, in trance, continued: "Ann is saying that there is something wrong with a light". Now as it happened the bulb in my study burned out the previous night when I was about to finish work and go to bed. I had made a mental note to buy a new 250 watt bulb but had not yet done so. I told Albert Best that my study lamp had gone out. Now this coincidence was a perfectly good explanation of what he claimed Ann had said, "Something wrong with a light". There was a pause and silence for almost half a minute. "No. This is not the light she is talking about. She says that the light could be dangerous." Another pause, then, "Would you please," she says, "check the lights on your car when you leave here. There is something wrong with one of them and it could be dangerous." Immediately after the session I went outside to where my car was parked and tested the lights. I found that my near-side side lamp was out. I also found that the wire behind the side light assembly was hot after the lights had been on for a few minutes.

Here was a source of danger, both of fire and the obvious

danger of driving at night without a front side-light. There was no conceivable way in which Albert Best could have been aware of this defect in my car. He had not even seen my car for weeks and in any case it was mid-summer and I would not have my lights on. In addition, there was the heating of the wire behind the light assembly. I am particularly impressed by this piece of evidence from Ann. It could not be known to any human agency, of this I am convinced. This is an example of something which is quite outside any kind of telepathic explanation. It is simple and yet it fulfills all the requirements of a non-telepathic condition. After all, pieces of wire and bulbs do not give off telepathic warnings. Yet there have been a number of good, well attested items such as this in psychical research. In one case known to me a medium has warned someone of a defective front tyre which was bulging on the inside.

It appears to be possible for helpers and loved ones on the other side to be aware of sources of potential danger and to try to give warning. This kind of evidence is very difficult to explain except on the survival hypothesis.

Reverting again to the items of evidence which Albert Best gave me at that afternoon session during pauses while healing patients; after the car evidence and while I was still in the small sanctuary he again spoke to me, "Ann says that yesterday morning you were looking for a blue vase." This again was accurate. I brought in some roses to place besides Ann's portrait and searched the house for a blue vase which I felt would be specially suitable. I did not find the vase and had to make do with a small crystal vase. He paused again, "Will you look . . . 'Just a moment,' she says, 'Will you look in the room next to the kitchen on the right going into the hall, you will find it there." Sure enough when I came home I found the blue vase in the spare bedroom in a drawer in the dresser. Ann must have put it there before she died. This bedroom is accurately described as 'the room next to the kitchen'.

One final amusing episode was still to come as the session ended. Albert Best, still in trance, called me aside and whispered to me, "Ann says that she is shocked at you. After all your years of Socialism and all her arguments with you, you switched round at the election and voted Tory." "Don't take it too seriously, she is smiling and saying, 'Just to let you know that I was there in the ballot box with you and saw where you put your cross, it's a little bit more evidence'."

My comment here is that not a living soul knew that for the first time in my life at the general election I voted for the Tory candidate. I had previously voted Socialist all my life and Ann had always been a rabid and enthusiastic Socialist. I may say that after voting I had no sense of betrayal or guilt, I felt that I had voted for the party which in the strange situation of British politics was actually the more radical at that moment.

Of one thing I am certain. I told no one, nor was I involved in any political argument at any time. What I did in the ballot box was a complete secret and yet Ann knew.

Finally, Albert Best said, "Ann is going but she wants to thank you for the two red roses which you put in front of her photograph." This was a separate small container into which I put two special roses beside a photograph in another room. Completely accurate. Thus ended one of the best and most evidential episodes with Albert Best. The critic may choose to explain one item or even two as fraud or coincidence. Yet all together there are ten items of separate evidence contained in this session and at the same session Albert Best was literally throwing 'messages' to others in the group of ten people there. It seems to me that no theory of conscious or unconscious collecting of items concerning the people at this session could be conceived. The knowledge of the defect in the electrical system of my car leaves me with the problem of how even a discarnate entity can be aware of this. Nevertheless it happens.

I can only feel a sense of gratitude and of Ann's closeness to me. No doubt if precognition is a feature of some communications from the other side this may be part of the explanation. It may be that lines of possibilities, including possible danger are known to those existing in a dimension where time is different from the time we experience.

As a minister of religion I am aware of a most significant change in the attitude of church people. A hundred years ago the fundamental question which orthodox church people asked themselves was, "How shall I face my maker and judge?" Today the question lurking behind the minds of church people is, "Have I a maker and a judge?" This is a fundamental change in men's attitudes. It is the transition from an age, indeed from ages of belief, of some sort, to an age of doubt.

The description in Boswell's *Life of Johnson* of the death bed scene with Dr. Johnson and Catherine Chambers, an old family friend is typical.

"I then kissed her. She told me that to part was the greatest pain she had ever felt and that she hoped we should meet again in a better place. I expressed, with swelled eyes, and great emotion of tenderness the same hopes. We kissed, and parted. I humbly hope to meet again and to part no more."

This account is over 200 years old. It could equally have been written by any orthodox believer right up to 1914. The account of Boswell shows a sincere and dignified attitude on the part of Dr. Johnson. There is little separating him from the best in pre-Christian attitudes to death such as we find in Cicero *On Old Age* and Plato's *Phaedo*. Victorian Christianity brought sentimentality and absurdity. "The Sweet Bye and Bye" typified all that was worst in the pre-1914 attitude to death. The corollary of 'The Sweet Bye and Bye' was an almost total lack of interest in the 'Here and Now' as it affected other human beings.

There is a dialectical pattern about the Christian attitude to death. If the thesis is 'The Sweet Bye and Bye' then the antithesis is the radical theology which proclaims the 'Death of God' and has no time for after life beliefs. Christians they say, ought to be concerned with authentic living now, with the problems of human need and political challenge. The question of an existence after death should not concern us. With every sympathy towards this attitude, I think it is wrong. A new synthesis in the dialectic of religious experience is required. While it must include the best in social concern and political involvement, this is not enough. The plain simple question which has been relegated to the basement of religious discussion must be aired. What happens after death?

If I dared to announce a sermon or discussion on the question "What happens after death?" I would be considered by my colleagues to be in bad taste, and by my congregation to have become a Christadelphian or to be going 'off my head'. The standard attitude or evasion of my colleagues in the ministry is to repeat the phrase which is constantly used. Eternal life is a quality to be entered into here and now. All very true! I agree but I cannot see that this in any way invalidates the question, 'What happens after death?' Do we survive the change called bodily death?

In this secular age the most recent figures I can find on the state of mind of people in the British Isles to the question of survival are interesting. In Gallup Poll's Television and Religion Survey of 1964 the figures for those who believe in an after life are as follows: 74% of Roman Catholics, 56% of Free church people and 49% of Anglicans. These figures are for 'paper' membership, those who nominally adhere to one or other church. For regular attenders, the figures are, Roman Catholics 88%, Free Church 86%, Anglicans 85%. I can see no reason why my Church of Scotland should be any better in percentage than the Church of England. This means that 15% of my regular worshippers go through a charade. When the crunch comes and bereavement strikes, their lives collapse. This is no theory derived from statistics. I once had the experience of burying the wife of an elder who had completed forty years' service as elder and church worker. In the car returning from the funeral service we were alone. He turned to me and spoke the most pathetic words I ever hope to hear, "Minister, do you think there is a chance?" He meant a chance that he might ever be reunited with the person who had shared over fifty years of his life. That man spoke for millions whose hearts break in silence. It is utterly trivial in the face of such simple misery to speak of eternal life now or concern with race relations or better housing. That man wanted a straight answer to a straight question, namely, 'What happens after death?' The sermon I dare not preach because it would label me a fanatic or crank.

If this is the situation within the churches, what is the situation without them. Fifteen years ago, in 1955, a B.B.C. report seemed to conclude that 43% of its viewers believed in a life after death. It would be a guess today, but a fairly reasonable one, to say that 60% of the population does not believe in a life after death. The tragedy is that much of modern theology has allowed itself to be pushed from behind by this great unreflecting secular pressure. This to the extent of denying that Christian theology is committed to belief in a life after death.

The assertion that eternal life is a quality to be entered into here and now in no way disposes of the problem. The real difficulty and the reason for secular man rejecting 'life after death' has always been that 'he cannot think it other than absurd'. In an age where we measure galactic distances and fundamental particles the idea of survival cannot be 'thought'. It has therefore been largely rejected. We might say that from the moment that heaven ceased to be a place the malaise of disbelief in survival began to grow.

The real bridge between religion and the 60% of non-believers in survival has been ignored. It was never to formulate a Christian theology which ignored or denied 'life after death'. It was to restore to secular man what he had lost, the 'thinkableness' of 'life after death'. The key to this I believe lies in the field of what is collectively called para-psychology. Modern Christian theology has largely ignored the work of Professor C. D. Broad, Professor H. H. Price, Professor Gardner Murphy, each of whom has tackled in his own way the problem of finding categories in which to 'think' survival. Some of their theories are daring, courageous and strange, but they are challenging. This can be said for each of these men. Their work represents a lifetime of study by first class philosophers on the problem of survival.

The question raised by mediumship of the quality which has been described in this book, the compelling force of the realisation that Ann has been present to me in a character-istic, dramatic way, all this cannot be set aside as vaguely embarrassing. Professor Butterworth once said of early Christianity that it survived because it 'out-thought the pagan world'. This is precisely what it is called upon to do today. To out-think the secular world and not to be pushed into categories of secular thought by its pressures.

16

I am conscious as I read what has been written and spoken by my fellow Christians of a pervading sense of arrogance towards almost all that lies outside the main stream of Christian thinking. Immortality is described by orthodox Christian writers as a kind of diminishing of man's potential. A deficient concept of God's love and purpose. Immortality, as defined by Christian theology is to go on, endlessly and aimlessly. It is really too modest for it carries the concepts of this life into the realm of God's purposes. In short, the general criticism of immortality is that it is a Greek concept which has no place in the Christian hope of Eternal Life which is something far more splendid.

One of the standards by which we can judge the belief in immortality in the pre-Christian world is simply this, did it enable those who held this belief to live and act with more honour and dignity? Cicero's essay, *On Old Age**, is neglected reading for most Christians. Even E. M. Forster pointed out that 'too little intelligence' is devoted to this essay. It is in the two final sections on Death and The After Life that the best of pre-Christian attitudes from a first class mind comes to us.

The opening section on The After Life is more frank than most modern writing on the subject. "I will tell you what I myself believe about death. I do not see why not, for the nearer this comes the better I feel I understand what it means. I loved your illustrious father, Scipio, and yours too, Laelius, and I am certain that they are still alive—living the only life that is worthy of the name."

Cicero goes on to point out that his conviction of survival is not simply the result of his own logic and reasoning. He cites philosophers, "Pythagoras and his disciples, who never

*I am using Michael Grant's translation which appeared in the Penguin Classics *Selected Works of Cicero*, 1960.

131

doubted, that each of our souls is a portion taken from the divine mind." Then he tells us that he has studied the arguments of Plato's *Phaedo,* "I have studied the arguments concerning the immortality of the soul which Socrates advanced on the last day of his life".

That his belief in survival was also shared by Xenophon is clear from Cicero's reference to Xenophon's essay on *The Education of Cyrus.* Here the elder Cyrus is made to say on his death bed 'My dear sons, do not conclude that after I have left you I shall have ceased to exist. Even while I have been with you, you have not seen my soul; you knew it was in this body because of the actions that I performed. In the future, too, my soul will remain invisible to you but you should still be able to credit its existence just as you have hitherto."

That the pre-Christian world believed in survival simply as a prosaic and endless concentration of worldly pleasures is not borne out by the quotation from Xenophon which Cicero uses. Again, from *The Education of Cyrus,* "Again, the closest thing to death (as you can see) is sleep. But sleep is precisely the condition in which souls most clearly manifest their divine nature. For when they are in this liberated and unrestrained state, they can see into the future, and that gives us a hint (notice, a 'hint') of what they will be like when they are no longer earthbound by the human frame." Surely here is a hint of what St. Paul envisages when he says, "For we know in part and we prophesy in part". Notice that Xenophon used the same argument. The soul sees into the future in a limited way, now. St. Paul says, "We prophesy (see into the future) in a limited way, now".

"For now we see as in a glass darkly; but then face to face; now I know in part; but then shall I know even as also I am known." There seems very little difference between St. Paul's argument and the argument of Xenophon quoted by Cicero.

Cicero's final summing up of his position and belief stands as one of the most sublime utterances in the ancient world. "I am not sorry to have lived, since the course of my life has encouraged me to believe that I have lived to some purpose. But what nature gave us is a place to dwell in temporarily, not to make one's own. When I leave life,

132

therefore, I shall feel as if I am leaving a hostel rather than a home.

"What a great day it will be when I set out to join that divine assemblage and concourse of souls, and depart from the confusion and corruption of this world! I shall be going to meet not only all those of whom I have spoken, but also my own son. No better, no more devoted man was ever born. He should have cremated my body; but I had to cremate his. Yet his soul has not gone from me, but looks back and fastens upon me its regard, and the destination to which that soul has departed is surely the place where it knew that I too must come."

"To the world I have seemed to bear my loss bravely. That does not mean that I found it easy to bear, but I comforted myself with the belief that our parting and separation would be of short duration."

That is one of the finest, most moving and most dignified assertions of religious belief ever written. It can stand beside the loftiest of the writings of St. Paul. It is clear that Cicero believed in a life after death but not only immortality; he believed in a continued expansion of quality of life. We do a great injustice to pre-Christian thought at its best when we stigmatise their belief in immortality as somehow inferior to the Christian conception of Everlasting Life.

If a critic were to attack the orthodox Christian concept of life after death on the basis of the picture conveyed in *The Book of Revelation* he would find it comparatively simple. Here we find a description of the New Jerusalem with its precise dimensions, twelve thousand furlongs in length and breadth, its walls of jasper, a hundred and forty-four cubits high, the foundations of sapphire and emerald and sardonyx and the streets of gold. The dwellers in this after life are 'before the throne of God and serve him day and night in his temple'. Surely this is a static picture of what would, if it were true, be a very dreary state of affairs. Of course, we Christians protest that this is all the imagery of poetry and is not to be taken seriously. Whether it was taken seriously by the early church is another question.

My point is that if we judge Socrates and Xenophon and Cicero by the imagery of their time and then discuss it as an inferior concept of survival; then we too must submit to be judged by the Biblical picture of life after death. This might be embarrassing for orthodox Christians.

It is to Plato's *Phaedo* that we must go for the most detailed scrutiny of the problem of life after death. The *Phaedo* is a later work of Plato. The beginning and the ending are agreed to be authentic accounts of what happened. The argument and discussion on immortality may well reflect not only what was held by Socrates but the development of this concept by Plato and others in the first half of the fourth century B.C. In the *Meno* Plato refers to immortality and pre-existence of the soul as a traditional doctrine. In the *Phaedo** Plato sets out, with the example of Socrates, to intellectually justify this traditional belief.

The sheer impact of Socrates' certainty of survival is conveyed with unquestionable authenticity in the closing part. '*Crito*: "How shall we bury you?" "Any way you like," replied Socrates. "That is, if you can catch me and I don't slip through your fingers." He laughed gently as he spoke and turning to us went on, "I can't persuade Crito that I am this Socrates here who is talking to you now and marshalling all the arguments; he thinks that I am the one whom he will see presently lying dead; and he asks how he is to bury me. As for my long and elaborate explanation that when I have drunk the poison I shall remain with you no longer, but depart to a state of heavenly happiness, this attempt to console both you and myself seems to be wasted on him———. You must assure him that when I am dead I shall not stay, but depart and be gone. That will help Crito to bear it more easily, and keep him from being distressed on my account when he sees my body being buried or burned, as if something dreadful was happening to me; or from saying at the funeral that it is Socrates whom he is laying out or carrying to the grave for burying———. No, you must keep up your spirits and say that it is only my body that you are burying; and you can bury it as you please, in whatever way you think most proper." '

I find these words of Socrates have the effect of great music or painting. I am moved to tears by them, because this is not form or sound, as an art-form. It is life itself,

---

*I use here Hugh Trendennick's translation of *The Last Days of Socrates*, Penguin Classics 1954.

expressing itself as an art-form. It has the same ring of certainty as Jesus of Nazareth when he says, "Do not be afraid of them that kill the body and after that have nothing more that they can do." Or when he turns to the dying man beside him on the cross and says, "Today thou shalt be with me in Paradise". Each utterance comes to us with the calm and assurance of the voice of God and each time from someone looking clearly and unflinchingly at what we call death.

In the *Phaedo,* Plato grapples with the problem which has always been present. The 'thinkableness' of the hereafter. St. Paul alludes to this question of situating the region beyond death in *Philippians* 2:10 when he says, "That at the name of Jesus every knee shall bow, of things in heaven, and things in earth, and things under the earth." Also in 2nd *Corinthians* 12:2 Paul speaks of himself as being 'caught up to the third heaven'. Paul is not sure whether this experience was 'in the body' or 'out of the body'. Most commentators find this remark of St. Paul embarrassing, as well it may be. Out of the body experiences are not the kind of material which fits easily into Christian Doctrine.

Paul undoubtedly situates heaven or the various heavens somewhere up in the sky. Scheol or Hades belongs to 'the things under the earth'. This is about as far as Paul is concerned to go. Plato attempts to be more scientific. "Imagine someone living in the depths of the sea. He might think that he was living on the surface, and seeing the sun and the other heavenly bodies through the water, he might think that the sea was the sky. He might be so sluggish and feeble that he had never reached the top of the sea, never emerged and raised his head from the sea into this world of ours and seen for himself how much purer and more beautiful it really is than the one in which his people live. Now we are just in the same position. Although we live in a hollow in the earth, we assume that we are living on the surface and we call the air heaven, as though it were the heaven through which the stars move." Plato's point is that if we could ascend high enough we would see that the real surface of the earth is what we call heaven and everything we see here is marred. Just in the same way as everything in the sea is corroded by brine. Thus a fish has not seen a real rock but only one covered with seaweed and dulled by adhesions. It is on the real surface of the earth, which we call heaven, that our souls go after purifying beyond death. The virtuous go there immediately, the ordinary souls after purification and penance in the regions under the earth.

This is Plato's attempt, and it is a brave one, to grapple with the perennial problem of situating the hereafter. The orthodox teaching of the Christian church today is that men will be judged at death and sent to their final destination (except for the Roman Church and the case of those who must pass through Purgatory). The orthodox teaching both of Roman and Protestant churches is that until the Last Day the souls of both blessed and damned remain dis-embodied. They are at death sent to their final state, in the Roman church, via the intermediate state of Purgatory. On the Last Day there will be a General Resurrection and at that point the disembodied souls are reunited to their old bodies. The Westminster Confession says, "at the Last Day —— all the dead shall be raised up with the self same bodies, and none other and shall be united again to their souls for ever.

The obvious fact is that orthodox Christian teaching about what happens after death is as far removed from men's sense of reality today as in Plato's teaching. Both are attempts to grapple with a problem in the scientific terms of 2000 years ago. Men have never ceased to believe in survival nor have they ever ceased to be aware of the presence of their departed loved ones. What both Platonic and Christian teaching on survival have in common is that neither runs away from the problem. Unfortunately, this cannot be said of modern Christianity.

Professor Willi Marxsen, Professor of New Testament in the University of Münster, in his book, *The Resurrection of Jesus of Nazareth* (S.C.M. Press, 1970) has this to say at the conclusion of his study. He deals with the question of what happens after death. He quotes the dying words of Heinrich Rendtorff, "These last nights I have been thinking over and testing everything that we can know and everything that we have been told about what will happen to us when we die. And now I am certain of one thing: I shall be safe." Marxsen concludes, "If anyone thinks that this is not enough, my answer would be, 'There is far more in the words, I shall be safe, than in all the pictures which one could conjure up. I think that it is right that this should be so. For the believer must not be modest in his faith. It is the person who carries over to the next world concepts belonging to this one who is being modest, because he is making the next world conform to this and is thus imposing limits on it." Willi Marxsen speaks for the great mass of clergymen and I do not deprecate the sincerity of his convictions. For better or worse fifty per cent. of nominal Christians do not feel 'safe'. Unless 'safety' be the blanket of non-existence which it does not mean in this context, then it is not so. From the figures which can be gathered, the great mass of the population do not find that statement enough. Fifty per cent. of my members do not find it enough and twenty per cent. of my regular worshippers do not find it enough.

It is not the professional theologian in the rarified atmosphere of academics who sees the weakness of the church in relation to the question 'What happens after death?' It is the parish minister who visits his own flock and non-members alike in an industrial area. There I see that people do break up, become embittered and bewildered at the point of bereavement. Nothing less than a zest and willingness to face and out-think the atheist and pessimist at this point will do.

The attitude of the early Christian church to death was certainly not one into which the advocate of survival and communication could fit his theories. Even Professor Willi Marxsen recognises that the hope of the resurrection of the dead 'is at least in origin, not a specifically Christian hope at all. Its roots lie in ancient Persian ideas'. He might have added that this concept was also present in the cult of Isis and Osiris and of Dionysus, both popular in the ancient world. Marxsen goes on to point out that these Persian ideas came to be admitted into Judaism and although the resurrection idea was still a matter of dispute in the time of Jesus, it soon made its way. The Jews came to be convinced of the future resurrection of the dead and are still convinced of it today. He points out that even in Islam, hope of the resurrection is to be found.

It is also beyond dispute that both Buddhist teaching and traditional Hindu teaching, specifically in the Upanishads and Bhagavad-Gita contains a concept of personal identity continuing in some form beyond death. Therefore, the

Christian traditional teaching of life beyond death is one of many attempts to cope with this problem.

When in 1st *Thessalonians*, Chapter 4, Paul writes his famous statement of reasurrance about what happens after death, "We would not have you ignorant brethren, concerning those who are asleep, that you may not grieve as others do who have no hope" he is overstating his case. There were certainly Stoics like the followers of Lucretius who had no hope. But Paul must have known perfectly well that there were many who shared the beliefs (I might even say certainty) of Cicero, and Platonic ideas of an afterlife were prevalent. In fairness to Paul, it is possible that he was alluding to the widespread pessimism of the Stoics.

The Christian attitude to death of the early centuries was bound up with the expectation of the 'parousia' when Christ would return in glory. Whether the bodies of the dead slept for 50 years or 100 years until they were united with their souls in heaven was not an important question. The important thing was that it would happen and it might happen at any minute. Of survival of their souls they were certain. Communication would probably have seemed an unnecessary impatience.

It is interesting to note that Canon Streeter in his scholarly article on the Resurrection of the Dead in Immortality (Macmillan & Co., 1920) points out, "To reject the idea of a possible interval between death and resurrection is no doubt to abandon the form of primitive Christian belief, but it is really to return to its substance. All the first generation of Christians believed, like St. Paul when he wrote his earlier letters, that in their own case there would be no interval at all between this life and the entering into the glorious life of the world to come. Thus if we affirm that we too, at once and without any interval of waiting, shall take on our new celestial bodies, we affirm exactly what the Apostles taught would happen to themselves and to every member of the church they knew. The notion of an age-long interval between death and resurrection is an inheritance from the letter of Jewish Apocalyptic which the actual vital belief of the first generation of Christians had in practice, though not in theory, already discarded."

However, 2000 years later when no parousia has taken place, the skies have not opened to reveal the Lord in glory and the end of the world, now it is no impatience to pose, as Christians, not only the question of survival but of communication.

What the early church did possess, however, was something which the present church has lost: an utterly buoyant, dynamic certainty that death was not the last word. The theme of burial services, so far as we can gather from inscriptions and especially from the catacombs was rejoicing. The theme of burial since Victorian times has been mourning. This is the great divide which separates the two attitudes to death.

Here we must look at the source of so many examples of the early church's attitude to death, the catacombs of Rome. These huge underground excavations, if they were extended in a continuous line, would stretch for almost 400 miles. They are cut from the 'tufa' which formed the sub-soil of a large part of ancient Rome. A special order of the Christian clergy 'fossores' or as we would say today, sextons, dug these tunnels. The Romans were well aware of these miles of excavations and it is supposed that some of them were dug out by Pagans for their own burials and also for other purposes. It is probable that various sects apart from Christians who preferred not to burn their dead, and this would include followers of the cult of Isis and Osiris, made use of the practice of excavating under Rome. The Jews in Rome would probably also make use of this vast subterranean cemetery, for they also believed in burying their dead.

The earliest known Christian inscription in the catacombs is A.D. 72. The latest is A.D. 410. It is interesting to compare the symbols which these men and women of the beginning of Christianity put on their cemeteries with the gloom of Victoriana. One could describe the inscriptions of the catacombs as the zenith of the spirit of rejoicing before death and Victorian cemeteries as the nadir of mourning of death. The symbols of the catacombs are the Ever-green leaf, the Harp—the symbol of Joy, the Cock—the symbol of morning. the Phoenix—the symbol of arising from the ashes and of course the Hart—the joyful exultant life of the young deer.

Compare this with the broken columns, the skulls, the urns with dripping vegetation, the pitcher, broken at the fountain, the symbols of misery and sentimentality which date from Puritan times almost to the present day. What could be more challenging than the words of the Epistle to Diognetus, "They are put to death and restored to life".

What of the inscriptions? A father brings his daughter or the tortured body of his daughter from the arena and places it in a niche in the wall and writes, "Agape, thou shalt live forever". The world outside has witnessed the death of a young man, again probably in the arena. His family bring his body to the catacombs and write simply and with all the defiance which we would long to have today, "Terentianus lives"—"Constantia ever faithful, went to God".

The word 'grieving' as Dean Farrar points out, is rare. Where today could we find the certainty of this epitaph, "Marcus, innocent boy, you have already begun to be among the innocent". The Cross is of course absent from the catacombs, except as the Christ monogram, not the Latin Cross. The earliest Latin Cross known occurs on the tomb of the Empress Galla Placidia, A.D. 451. The earliest crucifix is 6th century. So that the early church was concerned with Christ as The Good Shepherd, The Conqueror of Death, The present friend and source of strength.

It is perhaps most of all in the glorious words with which Dean Farrar concluded his summary of the early church in the introduction to his 'Lives of the Fathers' that we should conclude, "They took joyfully the spoiling of their possessions, knowing that they had their own selves for a better possession and an abiding. They braved death because death to them was life. And so they overcame the world, and handed to us across the darkness and tumult of the centuries, the brightening torch of Revelation and of Truth".

17

On Monday, 7th July, I had a sitting for the first time with a medium, Mrs. Constable, from Aberdeen. I had never met her before and booked the sitting as Mr. Hunter, by telephone. I arrived a total stranger to this elderly lady, probably approaching her seventies. I judged her to be a woman of forthright nature with an undisguised Aberdeen accent. She began, "You are working on a book just now but I feel that you have got stuck. Leave it aside for the moment and tonight just try to relax and scribble down any ideas that come to you, for half an hour or so." Suddenly she stopped, as though interrupted by someone whom she could hear, but who was not audible to me. "What's that you say? It's a lady speaking, she says, 'Tell him not tonight because he has to go out tonight'." I replied that I had an afternoon appointment but that I was free this evening and intended to be at home. "Oh no!" was the reply. "She says you are going to get a telephone call which will change your arrangements in the next few hours."

Mrs. Constable continued, "There is a lady here comes —the lady who spoke just now—a lovely lady—very beautiful —especially her hair. She says, 'Tell him it was my teeth. She had trouble with her teeth. She is very quiet—shy. She does this to her mouth (here Mrs. Constable put her hand over her mouth) as though she used to hide her mouth or her teeth with her hand."

I must emphasise how completely accurate this description is of my wife. She had a shallow palate and gums. For years of her life, until she died, she was plagued by the problem of finding dentures which were comfortable and even wearable. All together she had four sets of dentures at the time of her death. We used to have a private joke between us. She would say to me, "If I ever come back to you after I die, I'll just put my hand over my mouth and say, 'Remember my teeth'." It is true to say that her teeth were a constant source of pain and embarrassment to her and she used to take them out when she was alone and if I came into the bedroom she would place her hand over her mouth in an embarrassed gesture.

The remarks about my going out that evening are of particular interest. Surely, this is a kind of precognition. I had made arrangements to visit members of my congregation (to make detailed plans for a funeral service) that afternoon. The death was of a particularly tragic nature. The young man involved, the only son of the persons I was to visit, had been killed rock-climbing. This tragedy lay very heavily on my mind at the time of the sitting. Yet Ann was able to interrupt the medium in a most dramatic way and tell me that I would not be at home that evening but that I would get a telephone call in the next few hours, changing my plans. At 12 noon, a few minutes after I arrived home, I received a telephone call from the parents of the young man whose funeral I was to conduct. The call was to ask me if I would mind coming out in the evening instead of the afternoon. The actual time involved was from 6 p.m. till 11.30 p.m., as I had to make a transatlantic telephone call and I spent all the evening with the parents involved in this tragedy.

This knowledge on Ann's part of the course of the next few hours and the fact that I would be involved all evening might be brushed off as coincidence; a guess on the part of the medium. Yet if it were so, it was a detailed guess because it also mentioned a telephone call changing my plans. The chances of my plans for an entire evening being changed by something of this nature are very, very slender. It has happened to me once in the last two years. I regard this as a significant type of evidence of a non-telepathic nature.

Mrs. Constable's description continued, "She thanks you for three things. Firstly, you were the means of helping her to the other side. Secondly, you were the means of praying for her after she passed on and your prayers helped her a great deal. But thirdly, and most important of all, you were the means of looking after someone after she had gone. That is the most important. You did this and it is and was always so important to her. 'This I want to thank you for most of all,' she says. And she brings a rose and puts it in your

142

coat. You would often talk together about survival and you had a pact that which of you reached the other side first would make a point of trying to provide the best possible evidence for the other. Well, she is doing this and will go on trying to do it. She says that you have been discussing her and the possibility of your encountering her in certain types of what we call dreams. Well, she says, 'Watch out!' She will come to you one night in sleep but it will be no ordinary dream. You will know vividly that she has been with you, just wait for it."

"She shows me a silver tea service, teapot, hot water jug, sugar and cream. She mentions that she was specially proud of it. You gave it to her for a special occasion. You must get the clock mended. Don't get into trouble again by being late. She wants to say again how happy she is that you handled everything so well, but again most of all that you shouldered the responsibilities. She smiles now and says, 'Will you tell him my teeth are all right now'. She hugs you so possessively and points to the beard you have. 'Something different,' she says. She says that you are going to be aware of physical things happening in the home. Things will move and you will wonder if your eyes and ears are playing you false.

"Sir," said Mrs. Constable, "have you bought a new suit recently—I mean in the last few days, because she says that she was with you when you picked the new suit and she prompted you to choose it. Now she is telling me that she was with you and she listened in to a conversation you had recently with one or two other friends of yours. You spoke about survival and they thought your ideas were a little mad. At least that's the impression you got. But after you left them she waited and heard the end of the discussion. The stout one said, 'Well, in every other way he seems quite sound, and more down to earth than any minister I know.' Watch! You have sown a seed there. They will bring the subject up again to you.

Now your lady comes and puts her arms around you and says, 'We are coming around to another anniversary—in September. You will give me flowers, just as you always did and we would always arrange to go out somewhere. I will be there with you when it comes again'."

Then followed a memory of Ann's passing. "When I

143

passed over I was so tired. I felt that my body was so pain-ridden and utterly used up. It was just a shell of me. I watched you weep over me and I felt that my only regret would be leaving you, not getting rid of my body as it was. Now I am so happy. Tell him I'll be with him in September. As she goes she is weeping a little, she is just overcome with emotion at this reunion." I would like to consider some of the evidence so far.

I have dealt with the fact of the telephone call which was so startlingly correct. From this point Mrs. Constable listed three items for which Ann thanked me. My helping her to the other side. This in a very special sense I can claim to have done (see the description of Ann's death). Praying for her. This again I did, most emphatically, in spite of the fact that my church discourages prayers for the dead. The third point is the most evidential. I did take up the responsibility of Ann's mother and sister. Both needed a great deal of help and Ann worried a lot about them before she died. I made a point of travelling the ten miles to visit them twice each week since Ann's death and have been responsible for their problems in a practical way. No matter how busy I have been with church affairs, I have regarded this responsibility as a priority.

This is clearly stated, "You were the means of looking after someone after she was gone".

The pact between us that whichever reached the other side first would make an effort to provide the best of evidence. This is true, but not unusual.

The silver tea service was a special treasure of Ann's. I gave it to her for an anniversary present.

The clock ought to be repaired. This failure of my alarm clock had me in serious trouble two days previously.

I bought a new suit a week previously. Oddly enough I did not intend to buy a suit. I can honestly say I bought it on a whim, as though a voice said, "Go on! be a devil, buy it". It was a rather bright shepherd's tartan cloth and as I chose it I said to myself, 'Well, at least Ann would have liked it'.

The conversation with one or two friends is interesting. I did have an argument about survival four days earlier, in a club, with three friends. One of them could certainly be described as stout. I decided after this piece of evidence to 'stick my neck out' and ask my friend of the trio who was described as 'stout' if he and his two friends had commented on my remarks about survival after I left them. This was his reply: "Well," we said, "he seems a bit cracked on this," and I said, "In every other respect he is sound and more down to earth than most people and there it is." I left my friend with the feeling that he will bring this subject up again.

My comment on this is that if Ann is a creation of my imagination, she appears to be a very curious one. She claims to have a kind of volition of her own. This remark that she waited behind to hear the end of a conversation after I had gone and her accurate report of the ending of the conversation is very impressive. Either a part of my own personality is capable of remaining and listening to the end of a conversation after I have gone, unknown to me, then this part of my personality assigns the information it has subconsciously acquired to another dramatic creation—Ann—or the invisible presence of Ann was there from this other dimension and, for a time at any rate, she is drawn in a loving concern to share in my activities. This same loving concern is capable (I don't know how) of warning me of a danger in my car, unknown to any human agent.

The reference to her body being worn out and pain-ridden, just a shell of her former self, has been totally consistent with almost every medium I have interviewed. The reference to our anniversary in September was accurate (19th September) and the fact that we never missed going out together and of course I always bought her flowers.

The point was then made that I would be aware of physical phenomena in the home. Three days later as I finished dressing for the funeral of the young man so tragically killed mountain climbing, a rather curious thing happened.

I was putting in cuff-links, standing in the hall which was clear and brightly lit. There was no one else in the house. Suddenly my attention was directed to a large fifteen inch tall pottery vase which Ann had made herself on a potter's wheel. It stood on a solid oak cabinet. My attention was drawn to this vase by a loud crack. As I looked at the vase it began to rock in a semi-circular orbit which widened until the top of the vase was moving in a radius of a six-inch circle. This vase had never moved in my experience before. The oak cabinet was absolutely solid. There was no vibration of any kind, indeed no possible vibration could have produced this effect. It was the effect of an unseen hand slowly moving the vase from the top in a circular motion. Gradually the radius of the circle diminished and the vase became still again.

I watched the whole incident from about twelve feet away. I can testify that nothing even resembling this has ever happened to me before.

I am well aware that this is an unverifiable anecdote which the critic may discount. He may even find in this the straw that breaks the camel's back and consider me an unreliable witness on account of my description of what happened. I do not offer it as evidence of the nature of mental mediumship. It will have to remain among the growing mass of unverifiable anecdotes connected with psychical research. I can only say that it happened and Ann claimed that it would happen.

I am always diffident and unsure of the value which I ought to place on unverifiable accounts of physical phenomena. One could collect a volume of such experiences and they always suggest to me the words of Othello, 'I could a tale unfold'. My own reaction has always been to doubt the reliability of such tales. For example, a close friend of mine lost his wrist-watch in a hotel in the south of England. Six weeks later he awakened one morning conscious of a burning sensation on his chest. He found his wrist-watch which had been lost six weeks earlier, in England. It was lying in the centre of his bare chest. He was living in Glasgow when this happened.

Another person whose integrity I value in every respect had this strange experience to relate: She inherited a gold bracelet of thin South African gold, three-quarters of an inch broad and worn very thin. It belonged to her mother. The bracelet was worn so thin that it completely separated when she was forcing it on to her wrist. She wrapped the two parts in tissue paper. During the night she dreamed that she saw her mother vividly. Her mother said, "Go and look at the bracelet in the tissue paper". This woman awakened with a sense of urgency. She went to her jewel box, unwrapped the tissue paper and found the gold bracelet re-united at both the broken ends. The woman is utterly sound and reliable and as she said to me, "I dare not tell anyone but you and my husband about this or I would be considered mad". Her husband corroborates the entire incident. I have a feeling that more of such anecdotes remain hidden in families. They are afraid to divulge them lest the sanity of the teller be held in question.

Finally, Mrs. Constable produced one of the most impressive items of evidence that I have so far received. After Ann's death I gave away all her clothing. However, later I discovered that there still remained one or two items which I had not disposed of. I had noticed that one of the drawers in her dressing table was stuffed with nylon stockings, some of them in cellophane containers, others simply stuffed into the drawer. I could have thrown them out, but since a few pairs on the top appeared to be in unopened cellophane wrapping, I assume that there might be quite a few unused pairs of stockings in the drawer. I therefore left this drawer undisturbed, intending one day to ask some relative if the stockings were of any use to her. Indeed, I was glad to forget about this drawer and probably put off doing anything about it. The contents were quite undisturbed since before Ann's death.

Now comes this interesting piece of evidence from Mrs. Constable. "Your wife says that there is drawer beside the window in her bedroom at her dressing table. (This exactly describes the position of the dressing table.) In this drawer are stockings. You have opened the drawer but you have not disturbed the contents in any way. She says, 'He just took a look at what was in the drawer and closed it again'. She wants you to listen very carefully to this. If you take out the stockings you will find two things. You will find a purse—an old purse—and in it there is only one object, her lucky penny which she kept for many many years. Take it and keep it. Secondly, also in this drawer under the stockings, you will find in a corner two rings made into one.

When I came home I went to the drawer which I had been glad to close up till now. I took out the stockings there must have been dozens of pairs. Underneath them all I found a purse which I remember Ann using almost twenty years ago. I hadn't seen it for so long. I opened the purse and in it was one object, not a penny, a half-penny, with a piece of the coin snipped off, so that it was slightly more than a half circle. I remember that Ann had been given this coin as a lucky charm by some of her work-mates before she left to be married. I doubt if I had seen it in twenty-five years. There it was, not a penny as the medium had said, but a half-penny.

Now comes the double ring—something which Mrs. Constable described as two rings made into one. This I could simply not imagine. I thought in terms of the kind of ring one would wear on a finger, but there it was in the corner. A pair of ear-rings, each composed of a ring of gold linking into a second and larger ring of gold. Two rings made into one—a double ring. Strangely enough I had never seen this pair of ear-rings before. This is not surprising, however, as Ann had a fair amount of jewellery when we were married. Some of it she liked and wore frequently, other items she never wore. This happened to be a pair of ear-rings which I assume she didn't like and to my knowledge never wore in our married life. She may have considered wearing them at some time. At any rate, there they were, not in her jewel box but in this drawer under piles of nylon stockings. She may have intended giving them to someone.

Here we have two items, not known, as far as human reckoning can approach, to any living person, but undoubtedly known to Ann before she died. Both these items of information were given to me as evidence, and in categorically clear fashion, through the mediumship of Mrs. Constable. I believe that both of these items are beyond what can normally be attributed to telepathy. They are also consistent with the keen, analytical mind of Ann as I remember her, capable of remembering and insisting on the kind of evidence which would satisfy both of our intelligences. How difficult these items of evidence are to transmit through a medium, I have no idea. I think it is probably rather difficult, if we are to believe the accounts of the Myers-Gurney-Sidgwick communicators. Yet Ann has consistently kept to our pact and to her brief; namely, trying to provide the kind of evidence which would be beyond normal telepathic explanation and which would help to convince others.

There is a moving and touching element in the conclusion of this sitting. Mrs. Constable said, "Now your wife says,

'Do you remember the day we met? (How well we both remembered that day.) 'It was suddenly,' she says. 'Well, equally suddenly you will one day be aware of meeting me again.' She is leaving now. The power is fading. She just cannot help crying a little as she leaves you. But she is so happy to be able to come through."

This memorable sitting has all the ring of authenticity and it contains so many concrete items of evidence. I would suggest that the critic analyse and consider well the contents of this account. I believe it to be a genuine communication with Ann and in no single item is there a flaw—unless it be the naming of the coin as a penny instead of a half-penny.

On Monday, 6th July, I had a short sitting with Mrs. Findlater of which the following is of interest: "Yesterday you received a call for help. This is your wife reminding you about it. It was a call for a Samaritan and it cost you quite a lot materially. It rather puzzled you—why you, when there were two more closer at hand. Your wife says that it was not chance, she had a lot to do with it.

"Again at 10 a.m. yesterday you were rather called in question. You know what it was? She says she never wanted you to rush and when you arrived you were rather brought up by a question which was put to you point blank." The two incidents are accurate. First the Samaritan call: At 2 p.m. on the previous day (Sunday) I was coming home through Glasgow in my car. I heard a bumping in the boot and I stopped the car and got out to investigate. I was wearing a dog collar as I had recently taken a service. I could find nothing loose in the boot. As I was about to get into my car again someone tapped me on the shoulder. I was addressed by a rather bedraggled looking woman of between thirty-five and forty years. The details are not important, except to say that she had come from London over the weekend. She had hopes of living with a man she met in London who was now in Glasgow. The sorry ending of her trip was that he had got drunk the previous night, beaten her up, taken her money and thrown her out. Whether her story was true or not, she had bruises and all the evidence of having walked the streets all night.

My first thought was to give her the address of a church mission where her problems might be sorted out. Something stopped me and I did what I would not normally have done.

I said, "Are you hungry?" "I haven't eaten since yesterday," she replied. "Right," I said, "Come and have a meal with me and tell me your story". She was hungry all right and over the meal I listened for over an hour to someone who really needed someone to listen to and reassure her. She was really at a low ebb. Finally, after a deal of telephoning, I took her to a Y.W.C.A. hostel and explained the situation to the matron. I paid for her bed and breakfast and gave her money for her journey back to London and a few pounds to keep her over the next day or two. It cost me quite a lot, relative to what I could afford, but I felt that for once it was justified.

The other incident mentioned. That I was called in question by someone at 10 a.m. yesterday. Also that my wife never wanted me to rush. On the previous day (Sunday) for the first time in months I was taking a morning service 40 miles away. I slept rather late and found myself eventually having to speed at over 70 m.p.h. on the motorway and I just arrived at the church door at 10 a.m. when the service was supposed to start. Naturally some of the elders were worried and one of them said so. Half-joking he remarked that he thought some of his colleagues would have to take the service.

The two incidents reported here are specific and neither of them is in any way everyday occurrences. I am aware that an extended telepathy theory would explain both statements from the critic's point of view. Nevertheless, I offer them as quantity of evidence of my wife's continued concern for me and her knowledge and influencing of me in helping this poor girl in need, or of a remarkable kind of telepathy which is taking place almost daily in my life.

18

On Tuesday, 4th August, after a lapse of over a month since I last saw Albert Best, I once again took my crippled member of my congregation for healing. As usual Albert Best was in light trance. Once again Ann interrupted and in a most light-hearted way commented on my activities. "You have been wearing something belonging to someone else," said Albert Best. "Your wife is laughing." I couldn't think of any article of clothing belonging to someone else which I had worn and I said so. Albert Best made a circling movement around his neck and became more specific. "Last night you wore a tie belonging to a young person who was killed recently. Your wife is laughing about the tie, it was a bit young for you and you also bought a yellow shirt to match the tie. She says you looked like a canary. She says you really have bad taste. You ought to have got a blue shirt, it would have been in better taste. She is saying this jokingly," continued Albert Best. "She is also joking about what you did last night. She says, 'Tell him; he won't be embarrassed'." Albert Best continued, "You went somewhere in your yellow shirt and this floral tie and you bought a meat sandwich and ate it outside and you also had three tankards of beer. She says you are quite right to enjoy yourself, you needed to relax."

Albert became more serious, "Concerning the young fellow whose tie you wore, you held his wrist watch recently and looked at it. He also asks me to say that he knows about his tie pin."

Now a few days earlier I had visited the parents of the young man whom I have previously referred to. They asked me if I would like to have one of his ties which had never been worn. It was a typical, predominantly green, modern floral pattern tie. The kind of pattern which I would have rejected normally as too young for me. Nevertheless, I decided to accept the tie and wear it. Both because I knew the boy who had been killed whose tie it was and since I realised that his parents wanted me to wear it.

"She also says that the other day you were very fussy at a function of some kind. You refused the wine which was being offered and asked for a special Spanish wine—Ti-ti-Pep—something." Four days earlier, at a wedding, I had refrained from proposing the usual toasts in a rather sweet sherry and asked to be given a very dry sherry, 'Tio Pepe'. A small item delivered light-heartedly, but another brick in the evidence.

I had bought a bright yellow shirt (again out of my usual taste) to go with the tie. I wore them both the previous evening when I went out to a cricket match. During the evening I went into the club house and bought a meat sandwich. Again this is something I had not done in the last year, as I normally avoid eating sandwiches outside. I suddenly felt hungry and bought a meat sandwich. I also drank three tankards of beer during the evening while watching the cricket match.

It is also true that a few days earlier, at the home of the young fellow who had been killed recently, I was shown the wrist watch he had been wearing at the time, and handled it. The tie-pin reference was something unknown to me. However, I telephoned the parents and asked them if a tie-pin had any significance in relation to their son John. I was told that the boy's father had decided to wear his son's tie-pin which had a unique golfing crest on it and that he had worn it the previous day while playing golf.

Finally, Albert Best continued, "Ann is very light-hearted and as she goes off she says again to you, 'Enjoy yourself, you need relaxation' and smiling broadly she says, 'Yo-ho-ho and a bottle of rum.' You'll hear about that later she says. About the three tankards of beer she says, 'Tell him not to think I follow him all the time. I just looked in as you might say and was so happy to see that he was enjoying himself'." This ended what Ann had to say and the above was said in front of eight witnesses. I noted down the exact words as they were spoken.

On the veridical nature of the statements, my first comment is that as I write this twenty-four hours later, I have just been handed a present of a bottle of Jamaica Rum by a member of my congregation who has returned from holiday.

This is surely a reasonable interpretation of the laughing closing remark of Ann, "Yo-ho-ho and bottle of rum—you'll hear about that later." It is also a further example of a precognitive element in these messages.

I would like to analyse this afternoon's evidence further. I am impressed by the fact that the light-hearted mood is entirely consistent with my knowledge of Ann. Here is an example of a loved one attempting to convey a number of characteristic traits. The so-called dead can be full of fun and high spirits and in the right conditions they can convey this through a medium. I was feeling more relaxed and happier than for many months and I had been overworking for a considerable time. I believe that Ann tried and succeeded in conveying a typical mood which we often shared. Her humour was exactly in character and her remark about not liking the yellow shirt was again not unexpected. I honestly believe she would have, in better taste (and her taste was impeccable) have suggested a shade of blue. The atmosphere was one of light-hearted bantering about the three tankards of beer and the bottle of rum. We were all laughing and sharing in the mood Ann had created.

The criticism may be made that this is all trivial but the dramatic quality of a personality as remembered may sometimes best be conveyed by this kind of evidence. It can certainly be argued that this is evidence that people do not suddenly change at death. Why should they? If under good conditions a medium is able to convey a convincing, consistent description of a personality, it need not always be a sombre one. There have been times when Ann has been very serious and emotionally almost overcome in communicating. When from the other side they see their loved ones picking up and beginning to relax from the strain of bereavement, why should not the person on the other side convey this relaxation of mood too?

It might be inferred from a great deal of the details in this evidence that the so-called 'dead' are constantly looking in on us. But my experience is that this is not so. During the first six months or so after a bereavement when two people who have been very close are separated, I am convinced that this closeness and concern continues. Ann once said post mortem that it was as difficult for her to adjust as for me to adjust. This seems a very reasonable proposition if we assume that 'the dead' do survive. There is evidence that as we who are left on this side begin to 'take up the threads' again, this helps our loved ones to adjust also. I believe that while the bond of love is never broken between two people who love each other, that the need to be reassured of what the agent on this side is doing, becomes less as the months pass. The sooner a bereaved person adjusts to the closest compromise to a normal life that is possible, the sooner do we 'set free' our own loved ones.

If eternal life means progress and challenge and new discoveries in an ascending pilgrimage of closer proximity to the loving creative force we call God, then our loved ones have things to learn and work to do. One of the tragedies I see too often is over-grieving and pathological prolonging of grief. The knowledge of communication and survival can only serve to remedy this if it is conveyed and received intelligently.

At the moment I am concerned with a man who lost his wife four years ago. He makes a daily journey, summer and winter to the grave in a cemetery a few miles away. Four years after his wife's death he said to me, "I wish I were dead, every day, honestly I wish I were dead." The misery of this man's existence at the age of sixty-two is patently obvious. It is only an existence and his efforts at looking after himself are pathetic. Obviously he needs companionship and the hundred and one other things which a marriage would restore. Yet he is obsessed by the idea of loyalty to his departed spouse as something which must be the dominant factor in his life.

Curiously this man is in his own words 'not sure of survival' but he feels that he must 'play his role out' as he says to the end. He is an orthodox church member and attends church regularly. It is simply no good his doctor telling him that he should marry again. When I have told him this he has responded by being hurt. The horns of his dilemma are, 'If I and my wife survive and will meet again, how could I face her having remarried? If we don't survive then thirty-five years of loving relationship have no meaning and my loyalty is my gesture of defiance, at least I will keep her memory intact.' In such cases, and they are more common than we imagine, it is no good the church saying that your marriage was "until death do you part". Human beings have their own loyalties and while the marriage vows may be a contract "until death do us part", in the years of sharing and being together this relationship takes on another dimension. People feel that they were destined to meet. In the beautiful words of a centuries old French poet, "And to this end we twain are met".

It is my experience that in communications from loved ones which have the appearance of being genuine, widows or widowers are often told by their departed spouse to re-marry. They are reassured that there is no question of being disloyal and that their constant unhappiness is a source of grief to the 'departed' as well as to the grieving person here. The categorical reassurance that they must live a normal life and re-marry has in my experience been a saving factor in the lives of some people. I have knowledge of a number of such cases and my Spiritualist friends tell me that it is more common than people imagine. The idea that communication with our loved ones on the other side is an unhealthy attempt to continue a relationship which nature has ended, is a one-sided picture. It may be so in some cases. Equally in other cases it can have a salutary and normalising effect on someone in the category I have mentioned.

If we are to assume that the best type of communications are valid, then the first thing the surviving personality begins to realise is that 'loving' is not 'possessing'. It is true that the whole emphasis of Christian teaching is intended to stress this point and it is true that Jesus said that "in the Kingdom there is neither marriage nor giving in marriage". The difficulty is that people find it strange to conceive of the great lasting love relationship of their lives coming to an end. Quite often people come to me in later years, widows and widowers who would like to re-marry. They ask me what will happen after I die? If I meet my wife in the hereafter, and I have re-married, how could I face her?

One of the contributions of the most credible and intelligent communications from the other side is to add consistent and credible force to the Christian teaching of the nature of a true love relationship. In brief, they say that we recognise that there are groups of souls held together by an unselfish attraction. That loving is concern and responsibility for another. It is to desire the other person's good more than one's own gratification. Since the sexual element between male and female ends with the dissolution of this body, what is left is the attraction of true loving, which is sharing and caring. This relationship is completely compatible with a group of personalities attracted by mutual interest and concern.

If the second marriage of someone after his first wife's death held no real element of loving and attraction, it would be known on the other side for what it was. Both parties would see each other as they really exist towards each other. On the other hand, if a second marriage held elements of love and concern and attraction of spirits, then it can only add to the joy of the group of souls with which one's destiny is linked when they are together. The idea of competing claims of second marriages continuing into the life hereafter is dispelled as a pathetic failure to understand the magnificence of God's purpose for us. All this emerges from the best of mediumistic communications from the other side and its effect can surely only be a healthy one.

It seems to me that the task which I set out to perform is now complete. My purpose was to assemble and discuss the quality and quantity of evidence for survival which can be acquired over a period of roughly six months from the death of someone dear and close. I could go on for a further period of six months, no doubt acquiring and collecting further evidence, though I doubt if it would strengthen my case. This is a tendentious book. It begins with a theoretical belief in survival and communication and proceeds to show what happened in one particular instance when one's theories become existential problems. I believe that to acquire this amount of evidence of survival in so short a time would probably not be possible for most people. I was fortunate in so far as my wife and I shared a knowledge of psychical research over twenty-five years and latterly came to accept that evidence as strong enough to say that we both believed in survival. We were therefore agreed that when death parted us we would, whichever of us went first, and it seemed likely to be Ann, try to produce for the other one on this side the best evidence possible.

My part in this was to make this possible by having fairly

frequent sittings with mediums of known quality. The fortuitous part which figures so largely is the fact that I knew Albert Best, one of Britain's finest mediums. Out of this set of circumstances comes this book with its collection of items of evidence pointing so strongly towards the survival of the personality of Ann and I do not hesitate to say that I believe she survives and that we have done what we agreed to do.

Most of the evidence is of ordinary day to day things which happened to me, trivial incidents, like yesterday at a certain place you bought three tankards of beer and ate a sandwich and wore someone else's tie for the first time. The purpose behind the many examples of this nature in this book is to make it clear that Ann is saying, "It's true! I was there with you. I have never really been separated from you. However much you may fall into periods of depression, remember that I am close to you. This recalling of intimate details of my life since Ann died is perhaps the most natural thing that any loved one could be expected to do. It is therefore natural that the bulk of this evidence is of such a kind. I should imagine that if I had died first my principal concern in the first six months or so would be to reassure the person I had left behind.

It is perfectly true that many such items of evidence may be explained away by an extended telepathy theory and Ann was as much aware of this I am. Nevertheless, it is this reminding me of little details of my daily life which is the essence of this intercourse of personalities and the principal object of our attempts to reach each other was to minister to each other. The critic who finds in much of this book only evidence of telepathy may have his evidence and be welcome to it. Yet I cannot help reminding him that not so many years ago his predecessors were denying the existence of telepathy. No one has so far been able to demonstrate telepathy in such detail and clarity or with the lucid quality in which these communications come. One of the interesting objections to the telepathy theory, i.e. that a medium is able to tap in some detail my subconscious memories is shown here. Albert Best found that in spite of his desire to receive a message from Ann he was totally unable to receive anything for six weeks or so. If his mediumship is really telepathy, why should it not function a few days after Ann's death?

The existence of this delay of a varying period after someone's death before the best evidence is obtained tells against the telepathy theory. It may be that all mediums are in a nationwide conspiracy to create the dramatic effect of someone resting and adjusting after death. But I must say that the consistency of the fact, with different mediums, of the statement that Ann was still not able to communicate on her own but that my mother was helping her or relaying things from her, carries conviction. Later on my mother and father fade more and more into the background in sittings and Ann towards the end of the period is able to communicate herself.

Again, and particularly in the mediumship of Ena Twigg, there is a dramatic quality which it is difficult to convey in words but which was very real to me. I would have to say that she took on the personality of Ann and conveyed it in a manner which I find difficult to analyse in words. Other mediums also did this and this dramatic quality is something which, experienced at its best, is highly evidential.

Next, I would draw the reader's attention to the items which I did not know. Names of people known to her family long ago. Memories of family jokes such as the reference to the 'joke concerning milk', 'the ballet shoes', the 'Eiffel Tower model'*. With this I would place the reference to items which I was unaware existed in the home of her friends; the matchbox holder described in detail and others. Such items require us to believe that a medium such as Albert Best can tap the unconscious memories of Ann's relatives wherever they are. Then he arranges these selected unconscious memories of Ann's family and presents them to me as items of evidence from Ann which she says I will require to verify. I check on them and discover them to be correct.

This is not all. There is the unusual and yet well attested item which came in the presence of witnesses, of the defect

*During a telephone call from Albert Best in June, he referred to a Model of the Eiffel Tower which Ann was showing him. I later discovered that on the evidence of her mother and sister there had been at one time a model of the Eiffel Tower in her childhood home. This model had been lost or destroyed many years before I met her.

n the electrical system of my car. This light not functioning and wire heating up behind the panel was to the best of my knowledge, unknown to any human agency. Any telepathic theory of such an example requires the existence of certain information in the mind, consciously or subconsciously, of some human agent. Machinery does not give off information telepathically. The conclusion I am forced to accept is that communicators on the other side have some other method of being aware of a potential danger. In a different time-dimension this may be so.

There are also items here which it is difficult to fit into any category. Detailed items of precognition such as the knowledge of a telephone call which would change my plans and would come within a few hours. The reference to the gift of a bottle of rum twenty-four hours before I got it. There is also the case of the medium who telephoned me from forty miles away, with the feeling that she had to do it at Ann's behest. This awakened me from a sound sleep which would have entailed my missing the taking of an evening service. All this is a fair variety of evidence of different types.

At the same time it is fair to warn the reader that I have been pleading a case. I believed in survival and I hoped strongly that after Ann died I would receive evidence. I am not objective in this; but because I am aware of my desire to find myself in contact with Ann I have tried to guard against hearing what I desire to hear. All my sittings with mediums which were pre-arranged were tape recorded and I am satisfied that I did not convey information.

I have experienced sittings with mediums which were unsatisfactory in the sense that the messages were vague and could have applied to anyone. This happened on three or four occasions during the six months since Ann died. On such occasions I have switched off my tape after a few minutes and not troubled to record the sitting. One becomes able to recognise easily the medium who is simply filling in. Sometimes I have been convinced that the filling in was conscious and fraudulent. At other times I have felt that the hotch-potch of unrecognised names and allusions was not consciously fraudulent. Nevertheless, sterile and abortive sittings of this nature do take place and while I have not written down the details, it is fair to warn the reader that looking for evidence of survival has its setbacks too.

I have twice in my life-time had experience of materialisation sittings and on both occasions the materialisations I felt to be fraudulent. In any case serious psychical researchers are not interested in what cannot be demonstrated or reproduced for inquiry. Most cliams for materialisation have only anecdotal value. The person who was there claims to have witnessed it. This has little value as far as I am concerned. I want to be able to send a bereaved person on a course of investigation which will convince him of survival and mental mediumship at its best will, I believe, do this.

With all its limitations I therefore present the results of my period of six months or a little longer, of attempting to communicate with Ann, my wife. No doubt some of my church members and fellow ministers will be shocked. To them I would say, "Do not fall into the sin of arrogance which is really making your own experience the measure of other people's".

Others will be, I hope, curious to know more about the whole subject. To them I would repeat the enlightened words of the Church of Scotland's own committee on super-normal psychic phenomena, "Investigation is lawful—the church has welcomed the sure advance of knowledge in the physical sciences and is hopeful that the soul of men will soon be better understood.

Finally, to the bereaved and to those whose need is a question of the meaning of their existence, I say this: Your beloved are not further away from you, but closer to you. Sometimes only a thought—a prayer away. I believe that as I write these closing words, the living, vital, indestructible presence of Ann is somewhere over my shoulder now. She is laughing and saying words like these, "Thank God you've finished it, now you can get some exercise and fresh air. Get out and enjoy the August sunshine." I will! And from time to time we will renew our memories, Ann and I. This parting which we call death is simply "au revoir"—never—never goodbye.

Postscript

Almost six months have elapsed since I completed the last chapter of this book. My first inclination was to have the book in print as soon as possible and yet I delayed. There was the curious, uneasy feeling that it was not complete. In two later communications from my wife, there came the suggestion that I should put the book aside for a few months and then add a chapter summing up subsequent evidence. I also wished to know if the concentrated evidence of the previous months would continue. I wondered if there was present a psychological and emotional factor in the first months after the loss of a loved one, which tends towards the production of this kind of evidence.

Now, almost six months later, I have decided to add a postscript which I believe will complete this narrative. Two factors are concerned. One is the nature of the communications which followed the ending of what I intended to be the last chapter of this book. The other factor is my own emotional state a year after Ann's passing.

First, the communications of the last few months. At the beginning of September, during a sitting with Mrs. Findlater Ann referred to my book in these words: "You really have all the evidence you need for your book now. It has been a considerable effort from this side, you know. It is difficult for me to describe to you the problems of producing this kind of evidence and I have been greatly helped by others. It has meant for me that I have been much closer to you since I passed over: much more constantly with you, I mean, more than is really good for both of us. Now I have to make my way in this new life. This means discovering and understanding many things. It also means that later I shall be able to help you in more ways than either of us can imagine.

"You are also in need of a rest. The whole strain of writing this book and doing your church work at the same time has had its effect on you." (This is perfectly true. I had lost two stone in weight.) "You have not had a holiday this year or last. In fact, you have worked harder than ever this summer. Now you must relax. I shall not be communicating with you as often as during the last few months. I'll still be aware of what you are doing and I will be close to you from time to time, but not in the same constant way that I have been since I passed over. I have to progress and learn many things. We will always be held together by the bond of love, which will never change. Meanwhile, try to put the book aside for a while and we will give you material for a final chapter later."

About a week after this sitting I made my usual weekly visit to Albert Best's healing sanctuary, with the person whom I had taken in my car for healing, over the past months. I received this message from Albert Best, while he was in trance and healing. "Ann is here. She says that she will be going away now for some time. Like going to University. She has so much to learn. She says that she has met someone—Webb." I replied that I could not recollect this name as having any significance. Albert Best paused for a moment and then continued. "Webb—no that's not it. —It's the Webbs. Your wife is saying that you have a book in a cupboard, somewhere, written by them."

Then I remembered that among Ann's most prized books had been a two-volume history entitled *Soviet Communism,* written by Sydney and Beatrice Webb. I had not seen the volumes for a number of years, as in the course of removing many books had been put in chests and cupboards, which we had not been able to accommodate on shelves. Later when I arrived home I found the two-volume edition of *Soviet Communism* by Sydney and Beatrice Webb, among books piled in a cupboard. Certainly the existence of these volumes occupied no place in my conscious mind. It was only the added clue of the "book in a cupboard somewhere" which finally recalled the significance of the name.

At this time Albert Best, also relaying a message from Ann, spoke of "something about Pascal". Now Ann was also fond of reading Pascal's *Pensées*. The volume of this book which we had in a book-case was so old that the leather spine bearing the title was gone, and one could only discover the name of the book by opening the first pages. Therefore I consider it most unlikely that anyone entering my study could learn of the existence of this book by looking at the shelves. I consider the mention of this book by Ann as evidential.

Finally, Albert Best concluded on this occasion by saying "Your wife says that you must not expect to hear from her as often as in the past. She has done what she set out to do, now she needs to move on. She will still be with you in the love-bond, but not just communicating as often as in the past. She will be able to come from to time, just to let you know that she is there but you must not expect to hear from her as often as recently."

A fortnight later I was to be confronted with one of the most strange and unexpected pieces of evidence. On a Monday afternoon I arranged to take Ann's mother and sister for a drive in my car, to the coast. When I arrived at their home in East Kilbride, the weather was dull and it seemed likely to rain. We decided that instead of going for a drive to the coast, it would be a good idea if we went to a cinema in Glasgow. We chose to go to the film "Hello Dolly", a musical which was showing in a cinema in Renfield Street in Glasgow.

When we arrived in the centre of Glasgow, I found it difficult to find a parking place and I had to park about half-a-mile from the cinema we intended to visit. As there was ample time in hand, we walked from the parking place to the cinema, along Renfield Street, which is a busy shopping centre. During the journey along Renfield Street, we stopped to look at the window of a large gent's outfitter. We looked at the gent's raincoats on display and my mother-in-law suggested that I should buy a more modern style raincoat. We had some light-hearted chatter about how I would look in a rather modern teen-ager fashion of raincoat and we continued walking along the street to the cinema.

We entered the cinema about 2.30 p.m. and the feature film was about to start. After half-an-hour or so I remarked that this must be one of the most overrated and disappointing films I had ever seen. I found the film slow and boring and the whole story contrived. We all agreed that the film was poor so far, but we decided to see it through and we did. At the end of two and a half hours we came out of the cinema at the close of the performance. On leaving, we agreed that it had been an ill spent afternoon.

Outside the cinema, we stood for a few moments looking at the structure of a new cinema complex which was being created. This entailed the conversion of an old large-capacity cinema into a modern structure incorporating three cinemas, each featuring different types of film. We discussed the building and its features for a few minutes, then we walked along Renfield Street to the parking site where I had left the car and drove back to East Kilbride.

The same evening I returned to my home at 7 p.m. and spent the remainder of the evening working on a sermon. I went to bed at midnight. At 1 a.m. I was awakened by the ringing of my bedside telephone. I picked up the receiver and recognised the excited voice of Albert Best. "Ann has just come through to me. She seems light-hearted and elated and is telling me to telephone you now. I got out of bed to make this call. I apologise for ringing you at this time in the morning.

"She wants me to tell you that she appreciated what you did for her mother and sister this afternoon. She was with you most of the time. She wants me to tell you that first of all you changed your mind and drove to Glasgow with her folks. Then you all walked up Renfield Street and you stopped and looked at men's raincoats in a shop window. You were almost persuaded to buy a rather bright modern one—why didn't you? You then went into a cinema in Renfield Street. The film was so poor that you almost left after a little while. She says that she stayed with you for half-an-hour or so but the film was so boring that she had better things to do. She rejoined you when you were leaving the cinema. She says that you stood together and looked at a new building and commented on it, then you walked back to the car. She just wants you to know that at certain times she can be as close to you as this. She is very light-hearted and happy and sends her love to her mother and sisters."

This is the exact transcript of that telephone call which I noted down immediately afterwards. There are certain features of this remarkable communication which deserve comment. First, the exact chronological order and description of the afternoon's events. The compulsive critic will probably suggest that I was recognised and followed by someone. Such an explanation would have to contain a large number of co-incidental items. I intended to drive to the coast originally

164

nd changed my mind at the last minute. This excludes the
possibility of anyone knowing that I would be in Renfield
Street at a certain time. I had not seen Albert Best since
taking a patient to his clinic the previous week.

I have ascertained that Albert Best was in Kilmarnock on
the afternoon in question, almost twenty miles away. Anyone
following us would have to see us by chance and then follow
us undetected and yet be close enough to us to overhear
our remarks at the shop window. He would have to sit
close enough to us at the cinema to overhear our remarks
about the film. Then he would have to observe our
behaviour at the time we came out of the cinema. Since the
cinema was crowded and we were given three seats with no
vacant seats nearby, I find this explanation very difficult to
imagine. It also implies that someone would undertake all
this, then pass on the information to Albert Best for no
conceivable financial benefit but simply to deceive me. With
my previous knowledge of Albert Best's consistent integrity
can only find this explanation absurdly far-fetched.

There is an obvious critical objection to the above incident
as evidence of survival and communication. The useful principle of "Occam's Razor", that "entities are not to be
multiplied without necessity" must be applied here. Does
the account I have supplied here require the existence of a
"discarnate personality"? The answer is that of course, the
field of E.S.P. contains a number of more economical
explanations though each explanation is open to objections.
However, I do not claim that any one incident described in
this book should stand on its own. I do claim that at least
in the view of any fair-minded person a strong "prima facie"
case for Ann's survival is established by the totality of the
evidence presented. Human beings cannot leave existential
questions in the vacuum of suspended judgment. They either
make the leap from probability to belief or withdraw into
disbelief. This may well depend on emotional factors in
each of us.

As Cyril Burt points out in his brilliant essay on
"Psychology and Parapsychology" in the collection, *Science
and E.S.P.* (Routledge and Kegan Paul), the formula of the
doctrines of the Christian Creeds are "Credo in" which means
"I put my faith in". Aware, therefore, of the limitations of
most human assertions, I am convinced of Ann's survival

of death and if there is an element of faith in this assertion I am content that it should be so.

Since much of this book derives from the mediumship of Albert Best, I have one more incident to relate. This does not directly concern Ann, but it concerns the mediumship of Albert Best and must interest the reader who is weighing the evidence of this book. The event took place at the end of October, shortly after the incident of the cinema visit which I have dealt with in this chapter.

I asked Albert Best if he would come with me and visit a husband and wife in their mid-sixties, who had recently lost their son in a tragic climbing accident. The couple had shown a considerable interest in the question of survival and communication even before the death of their son. Since Ann's death they had followed closely from me, my account of what had happened. They were also among my closest personal friends. I hoped that Albert Best might be able to bring them some unique kind of evidence of their son's survival. They both believed in their son's survival on the basis of reading and their experience of three previous sittings with mediums at my flat. I arrived with Albert Best one evening, and this is an account of the "sitting" which took place.

We had dinner and sat chatting in the sitting room around the fire. Albert Best did not attempt to go into trance. He simply sat in an easy chair and took off his watch and put his keys and coins on the table. It is a curious feature of his mediumship that he claims that any metal objects on his person inhibits his mediumship.

Soon Albert Best claimed that he was aware of John, the deceased son of the couple we were visiting, being present. He referred to some details of a conversation which had taken place before we arrived and various other items of evidence of a minor character. The main and important item of evidence I shall describe in detail, since I consider it unique in its evidential value. It is the incident of the Postcard and Anthem-Book and I consider it to be among the best examples of Albert Best's mediumship.

First of all, Albert Best referred to a book, the nature of which he seemed uncertain. He felt that the book he wished to find as evidence was in the room. After an abortive attempt to locate the book on a table at his right-hand side,

Albert Best turned his attention to the grand piano on his left-hand side of the room. In the corner of the room beside the piano about a dozen books of various collections of music, were piled on the floor against the wall. Albert Best was attracted to this collection of books and asked Mr. Gemmell, our host, to hold up some of the books on the top of the pile. As he held up each book, Albert Best, still sitting some yards away, shook his head and rejected them.

"I want a book," he said, "with a picture in it—a picture —it looks like a Hawiian scene. There is blue sea, and a building and flowers." At last with mounting excitement he pointed to a book in the pile, near the bottom. Mr. Gemmell did not seem to grasp which book he wanted and still excited Albert Best rose from the chair and withdrew a book second from the bottom of the heap of books. It was an old Anthem book. He handed it to me and said will you turn to page ninety-six, there is something at that page. I opened the book and looked up page ninety-six. There was nothing of any significance, only musical notation. I thumbed through the book quickly and noticed something at page fifty-six. There, between the pages, was a coloured postcard of a scene on the island of Iona. Iona is in many ways a sub-tropical island in the summer. The sea has a quite remarkable shade of blue and the flowering shrubs could be described as exotic in colour. Also the outstanding building which stands alone, is the abbey. The postcard was such a scene—blue sea, flowering shrubs, and the building of the abbey. Yet it could at a glance be taken for a picture of a scene on Hawaii and it contained all the elements mentioned previously by Albert Best. The important fact is that Albert Best claimed that John, the son of Mr. and Mrs. Gemmell, who had been killed three months previously, was attempting to give this book and postcard as evidence.

The impressive features of this incident are these. Albert Best was never alone in the sitting room at any time that evening, nor did he leave the sitting room at any time. All of us can vouch for the fact that he did not go near the piano except to take the book from the pile. I therefore discount the idea of any kind of sleight-of-hand. The anthem book chosen had not been opened or used by anyone for at least two years. The only exception to this was John, the deceased son of Mr. and Mrs. Gemmell, who had been using this book in the year before his death. Mr. Gemmell remembers that about a year ago, he had suggested to John that he might improve his piano technique by practising some of the easier pieces in the anthem book. John was in the habit of doing this when everyone else had gone to bed. The postcard was one of a number which had been brought back from a holiday on Iona.

Both Mr. and Mrs. Gemmell are certain that they have never handled this anthem book or played such music in the last two years. It therefore seems likely that John Gemmell had played this piece of music on page 56 of the Anthem book and marked it with the coloured postcard of Iona, sometime during the past year. This is certainly the only reasonable explanation of how the coloured postcard of Iona got into the Anthem book at page 56. It is also worth pointing out that the musical item at page 56 would be of the type which a beginner would be likely to choose. If such an explanation is correct, then it points strongly towards the possibility that the discarnate communicator claiming to be John Gemmell attempted to establish his identity by producing through Albert Best, information known to himself and unknown to anyone else in the room or to any living person. I am aware that there is a certain amount of conjecture in this explanation. It assumes that the Gemmells had not used the Anthem book and inserted the postcard and forgotten about it. However, as both persons are highly intelligent and trustworthy, I believe this to be unlikely. In the context of Albert Best's previous mediumship described in this book, I am therefore very much impressed by the foregoing incident.

It is fitting that I should write the last words of this narrative on the anniversary of Ann's death. The last year has taught me more about myself than I had ever imagined. It has demonstrated to me that at least in my own case, the greatest emotional factor involved in bereavement is self-pity. The most painful of all recurring thoughts is "I shall not see her again, at least in this life". There may be twenty or thirty years stretching out ahead of me and I shall not look into her features or hear her voice or sense her perfume. The operative word is always "I". I am deprived of something. It is curious that although I believe that our loved ones are by the change we call death, also limited in their awareness of us, the converse thought does not occur. I do not find myself thinking that Ann will not be able to see me and hear my voice and touch me in the sense that she once did.

Whatever our views on the nature of the life hereafter, it appears that our loved ones may also feel a sense of shock and trauma, at first. For this reason they need our prayers. However, I must sadly admit that I have been sorry for myself a great deal of the time. Perhaps if we looked more honestly at the element of self pity in bereavement, it might have a cathartic effect on us. My advice to those who have lost a loved one is—observe how often such thoughts as "I can't go on", etc., occur. Notice the number of times that this ego—self—I dominates your field of thought, and accept that the Buddhist may be right; suffering is attachment to selfhood. This same process also causes suffering for the loved one on the other side, of this I am certain. It delays the progress of the soul whom we claim to love. We hold back our loved ones by not being willing to let them go "in love".

This must be my final thought and it is the note on which I wish to end this book. Believing in Ann's survival and in her communication with me and in our ultimate reuniting, I shall try to let her go "in love". If I can learn this lesson and embody its wisdom in the remainder of my days—it is enough for one lifetime.

Appendix 1

Prayers for the Dead

It is argued in this book that prayers for the dead are part of a healthy and indeed therapeutic rapport between ourselves and those in a post-mortem existence. From most of the evidence from the other side these prayers on our part are valuable both to the recently deceased personality and to the person remaining here in a state of grief and loss. They are probably of much more value than we realise.

Anyone who accepts the principle of faith healing, spirit healing or divine healing, believes that we invoke either latent powers in ourselves or Divine power or benificent forces. It may well be that most people believe in a combination of the above as operative. Prayer for the well-being of others is a request for healing or wholeness and such prayer for post mortem loved ones, or on their part for us might be defined as a form of absent healing. If healing operates at a distance it is reasonable to suppose that this distance is not so much a distance in space as a rapport in a dimension in which our spatial measurements do not apply.

This freedom from spatial restriction, at any rate in telepathy was clearly demonstrated by S. G. Soal in the experiments carried out with Mrs. Stewart who guessed cards at Merksem near Antwerp while the agents looked at the cards in London or Richmond. Mrs. Stewart maintained the same high rate of scoring at a distance of 200 miles as she did at 18-20 feet. (This is brought out by S. G. Soal in his lecture on the statistical aspects of E.S.P. in the Ciba Foundation Symposium on Extra-Sensory Perception, J. & A. Churchill Ltd., 1956.)

I therefore believe that Protestants in particular have a great deal to rediscover in the value of both prayers for the recently deceased and the knowledge that our loved ones on the other side are also concerned in prayers of healing for us. It is often argued by Protestants that the case for prayers for the dead is rather a weak one. This is based on the fact that the only scriptural authority for prayers for the dead is in 2nd Maccabees which belongs to the Apocrypha in the Authorised Version. There is also a passage in 2nd Timothy 1 v. 18, but this may be no more than a pious wish rather than an explicit prayer. I, therefore, quote a wide range of extracts from the Early Fathers and in later centuries in my claim that prayers for the dead, either formal or informal, have always been part of the tradition of the Christian Church.

1.   Tertullian (de Monogam) uses an argument against remarriage on the grounds that the widow prays for her deceased husband.

2.   Cyprian (Ep. XXXIX). We pray for the repose of martyrs and confessors on their anniversaries.

3.   Cyprian (De Mortalitate) (XXVI). Writing of the hereafter: "There a great number of dear ones awaits us— a thronging crowd of parents".

4.   Gregory of Nazianzus, A.D. 369. Prays for his brother Caesarius: "That he may have an entrance into heaven".

5.   Cyril of Jerusalem also writes of prayers for the dead.

6.   Augustine says that the custom was universal.

7.   Serapion, Bishop of Thmuis in Egypt, 350 A.D., in the Arabic Dedascalia, has a prayer for the departed to be used at funerals.

8.   There are the epitaphs from the earliest of Christian tombstones quoted in Bettenson's Documents Of The Christian Church.

Atticus: Sleep in peace secure in thy safety and pray anxiously for our sins.

4th Century Epitaph: Pray for thy parents Matronata Matrona, she lived 1 year 52 days.

Luther was very explicit in his attitude to prayers for the dead. (Gospel Sermon for 1st Sunday after Trinity, Lenker Edition Vol. XIII, para 28-29, says: "Shall we pray for the dead? We have no command from God to pray for the dead; therefore no one sins by not praying for them; for what God does not bid or forbid to do, in that no one can sin. Yet on the other hand, since God has not permitted us to know how it is with the souls of the departed and we must continue uninformed as to how he deals with them, we will not and cannot restrain them nor count it as sin if we pray for the dead. For we are ever certain from the Gospel that many have been raised from the dead who, we must confess, did not receive nor did they have their final sentence.

"Now since it is uncertain and no one knows whether final judgment has been passed upon these souls, it is not sin if you pray for them; but in this way, that you let it rest in uncertainty and speak thus: Dear God, if the departed souls be in a state that they may be helped, then I pray that you wouldst be gracious. And when you have thus prayed once or twice, then let it be sufficient and commend them unto God. For God has promised that when we pray to Him for anything He would hear us. Therefore, when you have prayed once or twice, you should believe that your prayer is answered, and there let it rest, lest you tempt God and mistrust Him."

Again, in Luther's letter to Bartholomew Von Staremberg, 1st September, 1524, on the death of Von Staremberg's wife Magdaline, Luther writes: "It is enough to pray God once or twice for her, because he has said to us, 'Whatsoever ye shall ask, if ye believe, ye shall receive' if we keep on praying for the same thing it is a sign that we do not believe."

For the views of the Eastern Church to the present day, which are also sympathetic to prayers for the dead see Timothy Ware "The Orthodox Church" (Pelican pp. 258-261.

As for the Anglican attitude; in the first Prayer Book of Edward VI there were prayers for the departed. The writer of the article in the Encyclopaedia Of Religion and Ethics points out that the Church of England neither commends nor condemns the practice and leaves it as far as private prayer is concerned to the discretion of its members.

The Anglican attitude also found expression in the writings of men like Herbert Thorndike, 1598-1672, who in "Just Weights and Measures" writes of the dead: "The church has always assisted them with the prayers of the living".

The Church of Scotland has largely been guided by the Westminster Confession which condemns prayers for the dead, but this Confession is now in the process of being relegated to the status of a historical statement (and good riddance to some of its intolerances). The same century which saw the flourishing of the Westminster Confession also witnessed the ridiculous situation in which ministers in Scotland did not even attend funerals.

The above will at least demonstrate that today the Protestant who insists on praying for his departed loved ones and believes that they also reach out to him in prayer, is no heretic, but in the mainstream of Christian tradition.

Appendix 2

Mediumship in the Early Church

Tertullian, or to give him his full name, Quintus Septimus Florens Tertullianus, was born circa 155 A.D. and died circa 222 A.D. is, with the exception of Augustine, the greatest of the writers of the early Church. From Tertullian we receive literally a cascade of information about the Western Christian Church at the end of the 2nd and the beginning of the 3rd century A.D.

Among Tertullian's later works (207-208 A.D.) is *De Anima*. It is, as the name implies, an inquiry concerning the soul or spirit, and it amounts to around 45,000 words. Adolph Harnack, perhaps the greatest of all scholars in early church history describes *De Anima* as the first book on Christian psychology. Today it would be better described as the first attempt within the Christian Church to grapple with the problems of parapsychology, for this is indeed what the treatise is concerned to do.

It is known that Tertullian became a Montanist sometime after 208 A.D. While the dating of most of Tertullian's works cannot be certain, Harnack is prepared to date *De Anima* as 207-208 A.D. As there is no reference in *De Anima* to lead the reader to believe that what Tertullian describes is not normal practice in the Western Church we must at least concede that there is a prima facie case for considering what follows as typical of the early church of the late 2nd century. This is a description of clairvoyance or mental mediumship.

"For seeing that we acknowledge spiritual charismata, or gifts, we too have merited the attainment of the prophetic gift. (Note that this is one of the few descriptions we have of what the early church understood by prophecy, a word which certainly did not mean foretelling events) although coming after John [The Baptist].)

We have now amongst us a sister whose lot it has been

to be favoured with sundry gifts of revelation, which she experiences in the spirit by ecstatic vision amidst the sacred rites of the Lord's Day in church. She converses with angels and sometimes even with the Lord; she both sees and hears mysterious communications; some men's hearts she understands, and to them who are in need she distributes remedies. Whether it be in the reading of Scriptures, or in the chanting of Psalms, or in the preaching of sermons, or in the offering up of prayers, in all these religious services matter and opportunity are afforded to her of seeing visions.

It may possibly have happened to us, while this sister of ours was rapt in the Spirit, that we had discoursed in some ineffable way about the soul. After the people are dismissed at the conclusion of the sacred services, she is in the regular habit of reporting to us whatever things she may have seen in vision (for all her communications are examined with the most scrupulous care, in order that the truth may be probed).

"Amongst other things," says she, "there has been shown to me a soul in bodily shape, and a spirit has been in the habit of appearing to me; not however a void and empty illusion, but such as offer itself to be even grasped by the hand, soft, transparent and of an etherial colour, and in form resembling that of a human being in every respect."

This was her vision, and for her witness there was God; and the apostle most assuredly foretold that there were to be "spiritual gifts" in the church. Now can you refuse to believe this, even if indubitable evidence on every point is forthcoming for your conviction?"

Here is a description of clairvoyance or mental mediumship which might describe a "sitting" with a medium today. Note the remark of Tertullian "for all her communications are examined with the most scrupulous care in order that the truth may be probed". There was nothing credulous about the attitude of these people of the early church. We might indeed say that here is a description of a Society For Psychical Research of almost 2000 years ago.

The text used in the above quotation is that of Fr. Oehler (3 Vols.) Leipzig, 1851-54 and the translation by Rev. Peter Holmes, D.D., F.R.A.S., in the collection of the writings of the Ante-Nicene Fathers, Vol. 15, published by T. & T.

Clark, Edinburgh, 1870, edited by Roberts and Donaldson, pages 427 and 428.

It is worth pointing out that Adolph Harnack claims that Tertullian himself never deviated from orthodoxy and vehemently asserts the orthodoxy of all Montanists. According to Harnack it was on the issue of more fasting, the prohibition of second marriages and greater separation from the world that the Montanists of North Africa differed from the Catholic Church.

Appendix 3

A Suggested Funeral Service

Nothing could be more designed to confuse and bewilder people than the orthodox Christian funeral service. Especially as it comes to the committal, "For as much as it has pleased Almighty God to take unto Himself the soul of our brother here departed, we therefore commit his body to the ground, earth to earth, ashes to ashes, dust to dust, in sure and certain hope of the resurrection to eternal life, through our Lord Jesus Christ."

To begin with the words, "It hath pleased Almighty God" may be well intentioned and might be acceptable in the burial service for an octogenarian. When a young man dies in a road accident and leaves a heart-broken wife and children it is bewildering and even offensive to suggest that "it hath pleased Almighty God". The idea that everything happens according to the will of God is a debatable theological proposition anyway.

Among the suggested readings in the Church of Scotland Book of Common Order there is "For a thousand years in Thy sight are but as yesterday when it is past, and as a watch in the night. Thou carriest them away as with a flood; they are as asleep; in the morning they are like grass which groweth up. In the morning it flourisheth and groweth up; in the evening it is cut down and withereth. The days of our years are three score years and ten; and if by reason of strength they be four score years, yet is their strength labour and sorrow; for it is soon cut off, and we fly away. So teach us to number our days, that we may apply our hearts unto wisdom."

The above is bad enough, but when it is spoken in a disinterested dirge, it is only likely to add to the bereaved person's ordeal and contributes nothing.

I have written and used my own funeral service for a number of years now and I offer the service as one of many suggested forms. Its merit to me is that it tries to strike the note of rejoicing and confidence which was so much part of the early church's attitude to death. It also avoids meaningless sentences in the preamble such as, "The souls of the righteous are in the hand of God, and there shall no torment touch them . . . they are in peace." To begin with the orthodox teaching of the church is that at death the souls of the righteous go to their ultimate destination—Heaven; there to be united with their resurrected earthly bodies at the final judgment. To say, "They are at peace" or "at rest" is a denial of even the church's concept of Heaven which is not a place of rest and peace but a place where the keynote is joy.

Usually in the funeral service the words which are always spoken as a preliminary are, "I am the resurrection and the life, saith the Lord; he that believeth in Me, though he were dead, yet shall he live: and whosoever liveth and believeth in Me shall never die." This is a great statement of faith by the early church, but the words were spoken in a context of the 'parousia'. Its corollary is of course that if we live and do not believe, we shall die. It would imply that eternal life is conditional on believing in Christ.

The church has always taught this but surely today, in a world in which we are aware of hundreds of millions of Buddhists, Mohammedans, Hindus, to say nothing of over a thousand-million Communists, this parochial view of God's love will not do. It is the extraction of a statement made by Jesus only in St. John's gospel, in the context of the raising of Lazarus. Remember, that St. John's gospel was in the opinion of most scholars, written probably at Ephesus between the years 90-100 A.D.

Professor Barclay points out that in this statement Jesus is not thinking of physical life but that Jesus was thinking of the death of sin. There is at least strong argument that such a sentence today, used in the context of bodily death, at a funeral, is out of place.

Here then is the funeral service I use: Jesus said, "Do not be afraid of them that kill the body and after that have nothing more that they can do." *Followed by this comment:* It is clear today that Our Lord means us to take from these words of strong reassurance not only "them that kill the body" but the accidents, the disease, the mishaps, which kill the body. Listen to the note of triumph! "And after that have nothing more that they can do." He is telling us today that even in the presence of Death, we are not to be afraid.

Again, let us remember that Our Lord said to the person dying beside Him on the Cross, "Today you shall be with me in Paradise". Notice His word, today. This makes it abundantly clear that we pass from this life through the gateway we call Death, to a joyful and happy condition. (The word 'Paradise' is a Persian word, it means 'a walled garden', a happy place.)

Blessed are they that mourn for they shall be comforted. (The following short prayer is offered)—

God our Father, give us strength for this day. We are sad because the visible presence of our beloved (John, Mary) is no longer with us. We are also proud of all that he did and brought in love and joy to others. In the midst of all our bewilderment and shock, help us to be able to hear Your voice within us, telling us that 'all is well'. 'All is well' with our loved one. Nothing which can happen to us in this life can separate use from Your great loving plan for each of us. Whatever else changes, Your love remains steadfast. You brought us together, so that we could love one another. Now, when we feel lost and separated from those whom we love, help us to know that You will keep us together. Through Jesus Christ, Amen.

For the Reading I suggest *Romans* 8, beginning, "I reckon that the sufferings of this present time, etc." I always introduce this reading with the words, "Let us remember that St. Paul wrote these words to a group of people who were in danger and who had lost their loved ones. There the Bible speaks to us today these words of reassurance.

The second reading I use is from *Revelation* 7, beginning, "And one of the elders answered" and ending with "They shall hunger no more". I introduce this passage with the words, "Let us remember that this passage is written in the language and imagery of poetry. It is a kind of poem, not an attempt to describe the life hereafter. But it tells us with confidence of the joy which God has set before our loved ones when they pass through the gateway of death."

Finally, listen to the words of ur Lord again. Jesus said, "Let not your heart be troubled: ye believe in God, believe also in Me. In my Father's house are many mansions: if it were not so, I would have told you." (The word mansions is

derived from a Latin word 'mansiones' which meant 'stages').
So that where our beloved has now gone, there are many
stages.

Listen to the words of Jesus, words of complete confidence
and reassurance for us at this time. We can base all our trust
in them. "Peace I leave with you, My peace I give unto you;
not as the world gives, give I unto you. Let not your heart
be troubled, neither let it be afraid."

Let us Pray:

God, our Father, who through Your gift of love, has taken
away the dread and the finality of death. Help us to know
at this time that every creature you have created is precious
in Your sight and that most of all we are precious to You.

Help us to know with calm certainty, at this time, the
things which You would have us know about what we call
death.

May we know that death, either for us or for our loved
ones, is not the end, it is the beginning. The opening of the
doors to a wider and fuller and more exciting life.

May we know that those whom we call dead are not
further away from us, but closer to us. That they come back
to us many times, to help us, to sustain us, and to reassure us.

May we know with certainty, that love is stronger than
death. You have so created us that when we love each other,
we cannot be separated by what we call death.

May we be strong in the knowledge that we shall meet
with our beloved (John, Mary) once again. That when this
time comes we shall recognise each other with joy and then
we shall take up the threads together again. This parting is
truly 'for a little while' but 'joy cometh in the morning'.

Therefore it is not in despair and desolation that we meet
to pay tribute to (John, Mary) whom we loved and to You,
our Father, in whose loving purpose we are held. We come
rejoicing! Rejoicing! in the gift of the personality of (John,
Mary) which you brought into our lives. Rejoicing in Your
promise of a certain reuniting; we leave our beloved (John,
Mary) in Your hands, till we meet together again.

We pray for James, Tom, Margaret, who were so close to
our beloved (John, Mary) and who miss his visible presence
so much. Give them courage and the knowledge that 'all
is well'.

Through Jesus Christ our Lord.

(And now a prayer of gratitude to God)—

Oh God, from whom come all the lovely and precious things in this life. We thank you with all our hearts for the life of our beloved (John, Mary) which you gave us. For all the love and courage he showed—(here may be inserted things personal to the deceased). Now since the time has come for him to move forward through the gateway of death into the next of the stages which Jesus said we would find in Our Father's house; we thank You that for (John, Mary) all the pain and sickness (or the weariness of old age) is over. Death itself is past. (He, she) has 'come through' and is now more alive than we are.

Grant that we may be inspired by the good example of those whom we are proud of today. May we take up our lives more bravely "looking ever unto Jesus, the author and finisher of our faith". We ask it through Jesus Christ our Lord, Amen.

The Committal.

St. Paul said, "If the earthly house of our tabernacle be dissolved we have a building not made with hands, eternal". This simply means that Paul was certain that we have a spiritual body which is more real than our material bodies and that it is not destroyed by Death.

Much as we loved the earthly body of (John, Mary) the real person was not limited to his body.

Therefore we stand now and salute the body which (John, Mary) used so well.

For as much as the earthly life of our beloved (John, Mary) has now come to an end, we commit his body, which he is finished with, to the earth (elements), Earth to Earth, Ashes to Ashes, Dust to Dust. (Pause). In the knowledge that we survive and life is eternal.

(Let us pray.) Oh God, we leave our beloved (John, Mary) in your gracious keeping. We know that he is safe. Grant to him Your guidance and Your light in his new life.

Oh God, You are leading us through all the changes of this life to the joy and challenge of the greater life You are preparing for us when we too pass through the gateway of death.

May we know always that we are each precious in Your sight, that we truly live forever more and that Your mercy endures in spite of our failures. Help us to be calm and trustful now and to take up our lives more bravely—for the sake of (John, Mary) who will still be caring for us. In love and care and tenderness to each other may we prepare for the time when we shall be re-united with all our loved ones.

Now we may leave this place—in Your strength and courage and most of all—rejoicing.

Through Jesus Christ our Lord.

Benediction: Go in Peace and carry that Peace into the lives of those who have no Peace.

May the Grace of the Lord Jesus Christ and the Love of God and the Fellowship of The Holy Spirit be with you and with your loved ones—uniting you always. Amen.

Appendix 4

Comments on the Report of Church of Scotland Committee on Supernormal Psychic Phenomena

As regards the members of the above committee it is interesting to note that it comprised seventeen clergymen, two medical specialists and two legal specialists and eight professors occupying chairs in Scottish Universities. Principal Galloway was Professor of Divinity in one of the colleges at St. Andrew's. Professor Baird, Professor of Biblical Criticism at Aberdeen. Professor Fulton was Professor of Systematic Theology at Aberdeen University. Professor Curtis, Professor of Biblical Criticism at Edinburgh University. Professor Paterson was Professor of Divinity at Edinburgh, and Professor Stevenson, Professor of Hebrew at Glasgow. By its nature, a committee covering a wide spectrum of opinion.

It would be unthinkable to expect a committee of 35 members to reach agreement on, for instance, the thesis that communication from post-mortem personalities was established. This would be equally impossible if one were to put the same questions to such a committee today. Indeed I have not made such an assertion in this book which is content to say that the evidence is such that I believe in the survival of Ann. The interesting points are the conclusions to which the whole committee are held as assenting to in substance.

These are under conclusions para. 12 beginning—"Investigation is lawful".

The recommendations of the whole committee are equally challenging. Para. 12: "The Church cannot dismiss these phenomena with indifference. Ministers may find rare genuine phenomena in the ordinary course of their duties, etc."

Finally, para. 18: "Just as Christians who have had special answers to special prayers are not excluded from the Church, so there is room in the larger life of the Church for Christian spiritualists whose special experiences have been sufficient to convince them. Such Christians should be encouraged to share in the life of the Church rather than to withdraw themselves from its communion."

Naturally, it would have been impossible for a church containing a wide spectrum of belief regarding survival and communication to do other than "receive" the report and the chairman of the committee, realising this, readily assented to this motion. It must be borne in mind that many church members would have condemned any investigation of psychical phenomena as trafficking with the devil, therefore, any attempt to commend the recommendations to the church at large would have split the Assembly. Thus the General Assembly of the Church of Scotland went further than the Anglican Church in that it discussed the report in General Assembly. In the case of the much discussed report of the Archbishops of York and Canterbury's Committee on Spiritualism, it was suppressed, although even more outspoken in favour of survival and communication.

The really interesting point is not what happened to the report in General Assembly, but that such a report, even with its warnings against fraud and deception (which are certainly reasonable) should be made by a committee of 35 persons with critical training and academic brilliance.

Commenting on this report today, one is conscious that two years is a totally inadequate time to investigate the problem of survival and communication. The committee became aware of this. What is really impressive is that when a committee of such distinction devotes even two years of its spare time to such an enquiry, they are united in affirming that such phenomena cannot be dismissed with indifference.

The question, "Do the dead communicate?" is today a question which is neither frivolous nor emotional. The mistake of previous decisions by churches to investigate has been in assuming that the answer can be given by a committee sitting for two or three or ten years. What is needed is a permanent bureau of investigation in which churches can co-operate. It is doubtful if any other body than the churches is better placed to do this.

REPORT

of the

COMMITTEE ON "SUPERNORMAL PSYCHIC PHENOMENA"

to the

GENERAL ASSEMBLY OF THE CHURCH OF SCOTLAND

26th May 1922

COMMITTEE, 1921-1922

Rev. Professor D. M. Kay, St. Andrews, *Convener*.

Very Rev. Principal Galloway, St. Andrews; Rev. Professor Baird, Aberdeen; Rev. Professor Curtis, Edinburgh; Rev. Professor Duncan, St. Andrews Rev. Professor Davidson, Aberdeen; Rev. Professor Fulton, Aberdeen; Rev. Professor Latta, Glasgow; Rev. Professor Paterson, Edinburgh; Rev. Professor Stevenson, Glasgow; Rev. Dr. Fisher, Edinburgh; Rev. Dr. Frew, Urr; Rev. Dr. Lamond, Edinburgh (resigned 29.4.22); Rev. Dr. Watson, Glasgow; Rev. Dr. White, Glasgow; Rev. Robert Alexander, Cupar; Rev. David Cathels, Hawick; Rev. W. S. Crockett, Tweedsmuir; Rev. Alex. Cross, Muthill; Rev. F. D. Langlands, Eastwood; Rev. J. Liddell, Advie; Rev. D. Macrae, Edderton; Rev. C. J. M. Middleton, Crailing; Rev. W. J. S. Miller, Edinburgh; Rev. John Muir, Paisley; Rev. W. A. Reid, Glasgow; Rev. T. G. Sinclair, Girvan; The Hon. Lord Sands, Edinburgh; Sheriff Scott Moncrieff, Edinburgh; A. K. Chalmer, Esq., M.D., Glasgow; J. A. Findlay, Esq., M.B.E., Glasgow; D. G. Lyall, Esq., Glasgow; David Russell, Esq., Markinch; A. G. Sanders, Esq., M.D., Lochmaben.

Rev. Robert Daly, Glasford, *Secretary*.

CONTENTS

REPORT

I. Purpose of Committee.

¶ 1. The General Assembly of the Church of Scotland on 25th May 1920 received a Petition on Supernormal Psychic Phenomena, and appointed a Committee "to inquire into the phenomena referred to in the Petition".

The Petition is as follows: —

"Petition—Rev. William A. Reid.

Unto the Venerable the General Assembly of the Church of Scotland, the Petition of William A. Reid.

Humbly sheweth,—

I, William A. Reid, retired Minister of West Maybole, residing at 24 India Street, Charing Cross, Glasgow, do humbly petition the General Assembly to appoint a Committee to inquire into the alleged supernormal psychic phenomena so much in evidence at present.

I give the following reasons for the Petition: —

1. The phenomena in question, such as clairvoyance, clairaudience, healing, speaking with tongues, are recorded throughout the whole Bible. The early Christian Church possessed these "spiritual gifts", and the Church was commanded to exercise them in perpetuity.

2. It is a mistake to condemn, without careful inquiry, those who exercise these "gifts", or those who believe in their reality. The fact that many people of undoubted mentality, in all classes of society, including ministers of all demoninations, have professed themselves convinced of the phenomena, indicates that the time has come for unbiassed and careful inquiry into the whole subject.

3. Large numbers of Church people, being convinced of the possibility of communicating with unseen intelligences, including their own departed friends, have lost interest in the Church and ceased to attend its services, so that spiritualistic meetings are on the increase, and Church services are correspondingly depleted.

4. Spiritualism is a method, not a religion. That is, spiritualists may profess any creed or none, be moral or immoral, orthodox or heterodox. Spiritual gifts are no more mysterious than mathematical or artistic gifts. To possess these gifts is one thing, to use them aright is another. It is asserted that there are now, as in Bible times, frauds and

liars who say 'the Lord has spoken when He has not,' and those who are mouthpieces of 'lying spirits'; but also that there are genuine communications from good spirits or 'ministering angels'. We must 'test the spirits'. If we believe the Bible, we cannot dismiss the claim with a jibe.

5. There are many societies throughout the world which approach this subject in a reverent, Christian spirit, and definitely accept Jesus Christ as Lord. Many faithful Church members in these societies, who are convinced that the continuity of life memory and capacity can be proved, are waiting some guidance from the Courts of the Church.

Modern psychic phenomena and Bible psychic phenomena stand or fall together. Hence it is believed by a large and increasing number that if modern psychic phenomena could be proved true the Bible would become to them virtually a new book, the experience of the early N.T. Church might be revived, and the kingdom of God advanced."

6. [*The last paragraph is omitted as being no longer necessary.*]

II. The Teaching of the Holy Scriptures

The Committee invited several of its members to examine the testimony of Scripture regarding phenomena such as are referred to in the Petition.

¶ 2. The *Old Testament* is a legacy from a thousand years, and it reflects a variety of experience and of opinion. When it is compared with preceding and with coeval literature, such as the Egyptian Book of the Dead, or the Babylonian tablets on omens, incantations, divination, astrology, and the like, or with ancient mythology generally, it becomes apparent that the Old Testament represents a triumph of rationalism over grotesque, absurd, and morbid theories of life. The possibility of mental stimulation by voices, by visions, and by other supernormal means is admitted; but the prophetic message has always to be clear, reasonable, and worthy of a righteous God. The prophets were conscious of the danger of self-deception and of false intimations, and the law sternly forbids sorcery, divination, necromancy, and similar traffic with the occult. Reasonable religion had often to struggle for its existence and often coexisted with relics of animism and superstition in the minds of the common people. It appears, therefore, that the Old Testament, far from encouraging occult sources of religion, explicitly forbids many forms of experiment with psychic phenomena.

¶ 3. The *New Testament* depicts the life of little more than a single generation. It teaches the doctrine that the Divine Spirit can and does influence the human spirit. The results of this influence are indicated in Gal. v. 22, 23: "The fruit of the Spirit is love, joy, peace, longsuffering, gentleness, goodness, faith, meekness, temperance." The interaction of Divine and human life is signified in the standard doctrines of the Incarnation and the Holy Spirit; and the exercise of Holy Communion is provided for by Prayer and the Sacrament of the Lord's Supper. Accounts are also given of extraordinary experiences which St. Paul encountered among some Christian converts at Corinth and Rome. These phenomena are ascribed to "spiritual gifts" which include "healing" and "speaking with tongues"; and they sometimes accompanied spiritual exaltation and fervent enthusiasm. St. Paul does not forbid this way of expressing high feeling, so long as it does not harm the common good; but he never suggests that imitation of the outward signs would generate the inspired feeling. Corinth was probably more addicted to spiritualism than any modern city. St. Paul, knowing the reality and intensity of spiritual forces in his own life-history, gives a reluctant toleration to the ecstatic behaviour of some Corinthians. "Five words with my understanding" are better than "ten thousand words in a tongue" (1 Corinthians xiv. 19). It is significant that his combat with undisciplined spiritualism forms the preamble to the praise of faith, hope, and charity (1 Corinthians xiii.), which he cordially commends as "a still more excellent way".

¶ 4. The Committee therefore conclude that in the normal life of the Church the "spiritual gifts" referred to in section (1) of the Petition are not an indispensable part of her equipment and service. The evangelic purpose with regard to the sick is being realised by the foundation of Medical Schools and the maintenance of Hospitals, as well as by faithful Prayer. The dissemination of the Scriptures in over five hundred languages is fulfilling the apostolic hope more surely than the effort to reproduce the speaking with tongues. The Creeds and the confession of Faith lay emphasis on other matters, and treat these temporary gifts as negligible accidents.

III. Modern Psychic Phenomena

¶ 5. In recent times attention has again been directed to some of the more mysterious capacities of the human spirit. Investigation of these suble experiences has been conducted by many groups of experts, notably by the Society for Psychical Research. The results attained in forty years by the many competent investigators of that Society have been surprisingly inconclusive. In his address for 1920, the President says: "As regards our positive conclusions and their value, I will only say this: I believe that telepathy is very nearly established for all time among the facts of Science, mainly by the work of this Society . . . During these forty years a whole generation of devoted workers has passed away. But what are forty years in the great possession of knowledge? Even though it were clear that four hundred years will be needed for the attainment of definite conclusions, we ought not to shrink from the task or falter by the way."—'Proceedings S.P.R.,' xxxi. p. 109.

¶ 6. The Assembly's Committee were anxious to avoid pronouncing an opinion on demonstrations which they had not observed for themselves. Many of the members have accordingly visited such séances as were accessible during the past two winters; and they desire to acknowledge the courtesy and hospitality they received from the members of various spiritualistic associations. Of the many varieties of phenomena, the Committee saw comparatively few—"the direct voice", "trance utterance", "table-tilting", "thought reading", and some others. A form of "levitation" was presupposed in the "direct voice" demonstration, as the megaphone or trumpet was supposed to rise of itself without physical contact from the floor, and touch the person addressed by the voice. The voice entered into conversation with various sitters; and the object of the message was supposed to be to convince the hearer that some deceased friend was addressing him, giving information which could not be known to the medium, and thus proving his survival after death.

¶ 7. The communications received were vague, ambiguous, and often commonplace. If a sitter were eagerly expectant and sympathetically uncritical, conviction might be produced. How the supposed spirit originated the air vibrations, which reached us as spoken or whispered words, was not made clear. Was this effect due to borrowing the larynx of the medium? or to materialisation of the vocal apparatus of the discarnate speaker? Even the use of the word "medium" requires justification. A middle term must have something on each side. The inquirer is on the one side, the person with psychic powers is a second, but who is the third? To postulate a familiar spirit, benevolent or malevolent, in an alleged spiritual sphere; to assume that this invisible assistant had the power to summon the greatest or the least of the Blessed Dead are assumptions which require, but have not received, any vindication by adequate evidence.

¶ 8. What impression have these séances as a whole made on those who assisted? Before joining this Committee some members had reached convictions as to the reality and possible explanations of these phenomena, and these members remain of the same opinion. Others began with impartial minds ready to accept any conclusion justified by sufficient evidence. As a specimen of the methods, the observation of facts, and the inferences drawn from the data, the following report of a Sub-Committee is printed in full.

REPORT FROM ONE OF THE SUB-COMMITTEES.

"The following report by seven members of the Assembly's Committee, who had special opportunities of making observations together, is now printed as an example of the material used by the Committee in coming to its conclusions.

"(1) *Special Case of X.*

We have been greatly indebted to a private individual, who may be named X, for permission to visit him frequently in his house and to observe there various kinds of physical phenomena. Because of our conviction of the honesty of X, and because of the extended opportunities we have had of observing his phenomena, we wish to state our opinion of these first and separately.

The corrective value of repeated observations of the same phenomena, under similar conditions, became increasingly apparent during the course of our visits to X, and, also, the difficulty of reaching a decisive conclusion, owing to the fact that he did not appreciate the necessity of experimental methods, and thought that these implied doubts of his honesty.

The chief events in X's house were the movements of a piano, a sideboard, and a table in one of his rooms. These movements were made in response to directions given by X, and in that sense showed intelligence. There was, however, nothing in them to indicate the action of discarnate spirits rather than of any other conceivable cause. The opinion of those reporting is divided as to whether or not a force other than ordinary physical pressure seemed to be operating. In this connection, it is recognised by all that any conclusion, being based upon observation merely, was difficult to substantiate. The hands of some of those present were always laid upon the objects that moved. X himself often stood aside, and on three occasions at least only members of Committee were in contact with the moving piano.

X's son, a boy of twelve years old, practises what some would call thought-reading, supposedly under the influence of spirits. He was carefully tested several times. On these occasions the results varied from unsuccessful to good. Even when his results were good, the conditions, in the opinion of the experimenters, were not such as to allow a decision in favour of his possessing special powers."

"(2) *Conclusion as to Spiritism.*

In addition to visiting X's house, we attended ten or twelve trumpet séances, and saw several demonstrations of clairvoyance (and clairaudience) and trance-speaking.

These experiences produced no conviction favourable to spiritism in the minds of those of us who had not been previously convinced. In addition, however, we received valuable testimony from two of our number, to the effect that their own spiritualistic beliefs rest upon past experiences, having a personal significance to which they can attach decisive importance. Those now reporting are, therefore, disposed to hold that only such personal experiences, if any at all, can supply the evidence for spiritism into which inquiry has been made."

"(3) *Alleged Supernormal Phenomena, other than those of X.*

Those of us who became practically acquainted with séances for the first time, in the course of our inquiries as members of the Church Committee, are not even satisfied that the clairvoyance, direct voice, and trance-speaking which we have witnessed were genuine supernormal phenomena at all. The published testimony in favour of some kinds of supernormal phenomena is so strong as to create a presumption that they actually do occur, but we ourselves, during these investigations, obtained no convincing favourable evidence. Indeed, we are of opinion that, generally speaking, the proof of the reality of these alleged supernormal phenomena and the investigation into them ought to be the work of highly-trained specialists, and that only inquiry prolonged over a considerable number of years, and conducted by the same investigators, is likely to have positive results."

"(4) *Possibility of Fraud.*

It must be added that most of us had experiences which we regarded as suspicious, and that a strong presumption exists, in the judgment of those members of our Group, that in some cases conscious fraud was practised. Trumpet séances especially, being always held in the dark, gave easy opportunities of fraud, which could not be adequately guarded against or controlled."

¶ 9. The foregoing statement is approved by all the seven investigators, two of whom were and remain spiritualist. The General Committee had other groups at work with similar séances. They had reviews of literature, accounts of automatic writing experiments, and critical investigation of a series of books on 'The Reality of Psychic Phenomena' and cognate subjects. The most favourable single verdict on the evidence submitted during our inquiry is perhaps the following: —

"As regards my particular conclusion from sittings which I have attended and my own personal experience thereat, I have come tentatively to the following conclusion: —

"That the medium makes statements in regard to deceased persons known to the sitter but unknown to the medium, which are difficult of explanation except (1) on the theory of communication with discarnate persons, or (2) on the theory that the medium reads out of the mind of the sitter facts which are not present at the time to the conscious mind of the sitter until the medium mentions them."

¶ 10. The preceding narrative may suffice to show that the members approached their task with independent judgment, that they formed their views after direct examination of experiments, and that they have exercised care in forming their opinions. The Committee as a whole has not been asked to endorse the opinions in the extracts given above, though the whole Committee is to be held as assenting to the substance of the following conclusions.

IV. Conclusions.

(A) ¶ 11. Psychical research has disclosed certain phenomena which have largely escaped the observation of traditional scientific psychology. Strange things do happen, no one can tell how or why. If the intelligence and will be made dormant, and if the eye or ear or hand be allowed to act without control, certain unexplained effects may sometimes follow. This admission is due, so far as the great majority of the Committee are concerned, not to their own direct observation, but to the published testimony of others. The genuine phenomena—real effects due to unknown causes—are comparatively very few; the great majority discussed in books deserve to be assigned to the category of "*alleged* supernormal phenomena".

¶ 12. Investigation is lawful. The Church has welcomed the sure advance of knowledge in the physical sciences, and is hopefully expectant that the soul of man will soon be better understood and more worthily honoured. But it must be made clear that the Church is in no sense dependent on the results of fresh discoveries: faith, hope, and charity will not be superseded by successful psychical research. The Church is not required to anticipate what will be the ultimate finding of scientific investigation. In the meantime no scientific finding has been sufficiently established to justify the Church in confidently accepting it, or adding it to her teaching.

(B) ¶ 13. The amazing extent of fraud, detected and admitted, is a disconcerting discovery for those who examine the history of spiritism. Believers in the cult claim a very small percentage of the professional mediums of the last fifty years as being always trustworthy. "There are a certain number of mediums of undoubted psychic power who, when that power temporarily deserts them—and it is, of course, intermittent—are immoral enough to fill up the gap with fraud." That is the avowal of a prominent leader among the spiritualists of to-day. The same authority says: "I think that to deceive the living by imitating the dead is the most horrible crime a man could commit." When the hope of

195

making money is added as a motive, the Church can do no other than follow St. Peter's treatment of Simon Magus.

¶ 14. There are other dangers apart from the dishonesty of agents. Mental irregularities are often induced by auto-suggestion or by fortune-telling, by unwise promises of healing which are doomed to disappointment, by the paralysis of intelligence and will, by self-surrender to unknown forces. Such dangers render it very imprudent for isolated and inexperienced persons to visit traffickers in the occult.

(C) ¶ 15. During and since the recent war there has been a natural anxiety to know whether there may be any possibility of communication with finite human personalities beyond the grave. Have the living any dealings with the dead? any obligation to their spirits? any means of exchanging thought or affection? any guidance to receive for the right exercise of this transitory life? Although the Church of Scotland in its doctrine has always maintained the existence of the Blessed Dead, yet in its practice at some periods it has been severely reticent in regard to the future life. It was not because the Reformers were indifferent to their kith and kin after death, but for profound and sufficient reasons, that they discouraged religious ceremonies at the burial of the dead. It is a natural instinctive feeling to mourn for the loss of friends; any kindness shown to their memory is pure, being free from the expectation of favours to come. That piety is defective which does not include a reasonable and reverent affection for our fathers before us. Pathetic expression of this enduring emotion often appears in the secular press.

¶ 16. The Church should provide some help to mourners in giving seemly expression to their feelings, in quelling within themselves the self-reproach for neglect, in preventing too deep and too frequent absorption in morbid regrets, and in cultivating a wholesome sense of fellowship with those who are gone forward before us. If the normal methods of keeping Christian communion were more adequately practised there would be less liability to have recourse to alleged supernormal means of communication. "If they hear not Moses and the Prophets, neither will they be persuaded though one rose from the dead."

V. RECOMMENDATIONS.

(A) ¶ 17. The Church cannot dismiss these phenomena with indifference. Ministers must deal with their own members as occasions arise. Ministers may find rare genuine phenomena in the ordinary course of their duties much more successfully than by resorting to mediums who produce preternatural phenomona on demand. A little investigation, however, serves to show that technical equipment of many delicate kinds, and expert workers in many fields, are essential for the proper scrutiny of facts and reasonings. The task of the Church is to cultivate the normal duties and dispositions of the Christian life. The investigation of these subtle phenomena cannot be satisfactorily undertaken by the scattered membership of a General Assembly Committee.

(B) ¶ 18. The attendance of Christian people at spiritualistic séances is open to serious dangers. Those who attend are seldom disposed or qualified to be critical investigators, and they may yield themselves to deception or illusion. Such meetings can never be a substitute for the exercise of ordinary Christian worship. The existing faith and practice of the Church are still the essentials of a Christian life. Just as Christians who have had special answers to special prayers are not excluded from the Church, so there is room in the larger life of the Church for Christian spiritualists whose special experiences have been sufficient to convince them. Such Christians should be encouraged to share in the life of the Church rather than to withdraw themselves from its communion.

(C) ¶ 19. The Assembly to invite its Committee on Aids to Devotion to endeavour to provide more fully devotional meditations and prayers which may serve to mitigate the anguish of bereavement, to soothe the grief of mourners, and to encourage individuals and families in cherishing the memory of their fathers with true Christian affection.

(D) ¶ 20. The Assembly to recommend ministers to give due recognition in public worship to the provision made in the ordinances of the Church for the reverent and affectionate commemoration of the faithful departed.

In name and by appointment of the Committee.

D. M. KAY, *Convener.*

Extract Deliverance of the General Assembly of the Church of Scotland on the foregoing Report.

At Edinburgh, the Twenty-sixth day of May, One thousand nine hundred and twenty-two years,—

Which day the General Assembly of the Church of Scotland being met and constituted,—*inter alia,*

The General Assembly called for the Report of the Committee on "Supernormal" Psychic Phenomena, which was given in by Professor Kay, Convener, who moved—

The General Assembly receive the Report, adopt the recommendations contained therein, and commend them to the attention of ministers and people, acknowledge the diligence of the Committee, and discharge it.

The Motion was seconded.

It was moved as an Amendment—Omit from the Motion the words "adopt the recommendations contained therein, and commend them to the attention of ministers and people."

This was seconded.

A Second Motion was moved—Receive the Report, remit the relevant parts of the recommendations to the Committee on Aids to Devotion, thank the Committee, and discharge it.

This was seconded.

The Amendment was, with consent of the General Assembly, withdrawn.

The First Motion was withdrawn, and the Second Motion became the finding of the General Assembly.

It was moved, seconded, and agreed—That Professor Kay and Mr. Cathels be added to the Committee on Aids to Devotion.

Extracted from the Records of the General Assembly of the Church of Scotland by

DAVID PAUL,
Cl. Eccl. Scot.